CASTLES OF
ENGLAND

Books by the same author :

Inns and Villages of England

A Second Book of Inns and Villages of England

A Guide to English Country Houses

Malta : Blue-Water Island

Odd Aspects of England

etc

Castles of
England

by GARRY HOGG

DAVID & CHARLES   :   NEWTON ABBOT

0 7153 4773 X

Printed in Great Britain by
W J Holman Limited Dawlish
for David & Charles (Publishers) Limited
South Devon House Newton Abbot Devon

Contents

Acknowledgments

British Travel Association : plates on pages 11, 13, 27, 29, 31, 33, 35, 37, 41, 43, 45, 49, 55, 57, 61, 63, 65, 67, 71, 73, 75, 77, 79, 83, 85, 89, 91, 93, 95, 97, 105, 107, 109

Ministry of Public Building and Works : plates on pages 15, 17, 19, 21, 23, 25, 39, 47, 59, 69, 81, 87, 99, 101, 103

Lincolnshire County Committee : plate on page 51

Leonard & Marjorie Gayton : plate on page 53

Foreword

A 'sermon in stone': the phrase is often used to describe one of our cathedrals. No less apt is the phrase 'history in stone' to describe a castle whose crumbling masonry bears witness to the story of the centuries of occupation, siege and change-of-ownership it has known as its fortunes fluctuated down the ages.

There are hundreds of castles in Britain whose origins date back nine centuries, to within a few years of the coming to these shores of William of Normandy in 1066. There had, of course, been castles of a sort—the iron-age hill-forts and the later timber strongholds enclosed by stout palisades—prior to the Battle of Hastings; but it was the Normans who established the castles of stone in this country: castles which are scattered far and wide throughout these islands. In England alone there are well over a hundred, few of the forty or so counties being without one or more.

Castles are found in profusion along the coastline from the Thames estuary to Cornwall, for it was across the English Channel that the invader was most likely to come. So, Kent has Dover, Deal and Walmer; Sussex has Pevensey and Arundel; Hampshire has Portchester and, on the adjacent Isle of Wight, Carisbrooke; Devonshire has Dartmouth; Cornwall has Pendennis and St Mawes. Nor are these all that could be named. They are found in like profusion in Border country. Northumbria has, among others, Bamburgh and Warkworth, Norham, Carlisle, Brougham and Alnwick; in the indeterminate and once savagely contested Welsh Marches there are Grosmont and Skenfrith, Chepstow, Monmouth and Raglan, and many more. Castles were built, too, in order to dominate certain strategic inland routes. Newark Castle, for instance, stands on the river bank where the old Great North Road and the Roman Fosse Way converged on one another and jointly crossed the Trent; in Westmorland, Brough Castle guarded the vital Stainmore approach to the Pennines.

Of the hundreds of castles that have survived the rough usage of the centuries, only fifty have been chosen for the present book and all these are in England. (Scottish and Welsh castles merit a book to themselves.) They have been picked from rather more than half our counties, and it will be seen that they differ as widely in appearance and state of preservation as they do in distribution. They range from those that now offer little more than a tantalising hint of the greatness they possessed in their heyday, to those that are still owner-occupied and maintain to this day the splendour that characterised them in their prime. They range from seaward-facing fortresses to monumental complexes of towers and curtain walls, gatehouses and barbicans, crowning steep heights that dominate the landscape for miles in every direction.

Some of them are no more than an outcrop or two of resistant masonry tumbled about on turf-clad earthworks that once supported the weight of noble towers and walls; Berkhamsted Castle would be a good example of this. Others, among which are Berkeley and Alnwick, Dunster and Arundel, Dover and Windsor, still present the appearance that results from generations, sometimes even from whole centuries, of devoted maintenance. In certain cases the castle has been occupied by the same family for all or most of the centuries that have elapsed since it was first granted to their ancestors by the reigning monarch of the time as a reward for loyal service in the field, or for some other state duty honourably fulfilled over a long period of time.

It should not, however, be thought that it is solely these owner-occupied glories that deserve to be visited: Dunster and Arundel, Windsor and Berkeley, for instance. It is true that such famous castles usually offer the visitor a greater wealth and variety of interest, for the buildings are more extensive and in a better state of repair, and house a greater variety of accumulated treasure than is the case in the lesser castles. But the fascination, if of a different type, is no less gripping among the many impressive ruins scattered about the country: ruins that still speak, if only tacitly, of the greatness that was once theirs and persuade the responsive visitor that their tumbled masonry, their battered walls, their roofless keeps and towers, have a story no less interesting and memorable to recount. Many of them were 'slighted' by the Parliamentary troops towards the close of the Civil War, over three centuries ago. Slighting was the deliberate mutilation of a castle by the victors; it varied from relatively modest damage to virtually complete destruction. It was designed to emphasise the complete success of the victors after a siege of greater or lesser duration. If the victors intended to make use of the castle for their own purposes, they naturally practised restraint in the actual damage they did. Other castles fell upon evil times for different reasons. You will become keenly aware of the individual tragedies that befell them as you look, for example, at Hedingham, and Nunney, Portchester and Framlingham, Grosmont and Warkworth, Peveril, Tintagel, Kenilworth and Conisbrough.

Some of the castles described here are privately owned and occupied; some of them are National Trust property; the majority are in the expert care of the Ministry of Public Building and Works. All of them are open to the public. Where the phrase 'standard hours' has been used in the information appended to each castle as to times of opening, it has been supplied by the Ministry of Public Building and Works, within whose jurisdiction the specific castles lie. The phrase should be interpreted as follows :

March - April	Weekdays 9.30 - 5.30	Sundays 2 - 5.30
May - September	Weekdays 9.30 - 7	Sundays 2 - 7

October	Weekdays 9.30 - 5.30	Sundays 2 - 5.30
November to		
February	Weekdays 10.0 - 4.30	Sundays 2 - 4.30

The times at which they are open are correct as the book goes to press, but these can vary, and it is as well to check in advance if a special journey of some distance is involved. At all these places you can buy, quite cheaply, an authoritatively written and illustrated guidebook, or at least an informative brochure. This will tell the full story of the castle and indicate special points of interest that you should look out for. This guidebook material is of course very much more detailed, with its photographs and diagrams embellishing the text, than the few paragraphs that face each illustration in this book. Here, an attempt has simply been made to draw attention to the merit and interest of each castle included, as a site to be visited, and to outline very briefly its major features and the highlights of its history. To explore these sites with the relevant guidebook in hand, however, is an infinitely more rewarding experience than simply to wander around with no real knowledge or clear idea of what to look for or where to find it.

There is almost always a small charge for admission; the money, of course, goes towards the often heavy cost of maintenance. So far as the castles under the care of the Ministry of Public Building and Works are concerned, a season ticket valid for twelve months and entitling the holder to visit as many sites of castles, historic and prehistoric monuments as he wishes may, at the time of writing, be obtained for 15s (children at half-price). United States citizens and Canadians can obtain these for $2 ($1 for children) by writing to the Ministry of Public Building and Works (CIO Branch) at Lambeth Bridge House, London SE1. Or, of course, the tickets can be obtained, direct, when the overseas visitor has reached these shores. The fifty castles included in this book, and the many scores of others, constitute only a small proportion of the sites throughout the length and breadth of the British Isles which the ticket enables the holder to explore. Indeed, a full twelve months spent in quartering the country, route map in hand, would be insufficient time in which to do justice to a mere fraction of the sites that await the visitor.

G.H.

Groombridge, Sussex

Berkshire

DONNINGTON CASTLE
(Off B4000, 1 mile north-west of Newbury)

In 1586 it was described as a 'small but very neat castle, seated on the banks of a woody hill, having a fair prospect, and windows in all sides, very lightsome'. Built in 1386, it was then just 200 years old, and so somewhat 'junior' to the many castles built by the Normans immediately after the triumph of William the Conqueror at the Battle of Hastings in 1066. Junior, but none the less most efficiently designed and built to command two important highways: that which ran north-south to link Northampton with Southampton, and that which ran east-west to link London with Bath. It stands in a dominant position on a spur of high ground.

Today, apart from the lower courses of the walls, the four round bastion towers and two square towers on the north and south walls, only the massive gatehouse stands. It rises to nearly 70 ft, flanked by two great drum-towers forming a barbican; between them, the first of two or more portcullises could be raised and lowered to bar access. The 65-step spiral stairway in the south tower is unusual in that it turns counter-clockwise, and an unusual feature of the north tower is that it once housed a dovecote. This was functional, not decorative—especially in time of a prolonged siege such as that which ended in the virtual destruction of the castle.

Donnington had a shorter life than many of its fellow castles, for it was involved in the fortunes of King Charles in the Civil War. Under the inspiring leadership of Colonel Sir John Boys its fanatically loyal garrison held out against a twenty-month siege that only ended in April 1646 when the king himself ordered Sir John to surrender with honour and colours flying. By then its curtain walls had been battered almost to ground level by the enormous array of artillery deployed against it; without its elaborate star-shaped system of earthworks which had been thrown up when the prospect of siege became certain, it would not have held out for so long. Though so much of the fabric has almost completely vanished as a result of that siege, scars remain on the flanks of the almost impregnable fourteenth-century gate tower: marks of the cannon-balls hurled against the masonry that still stands, a mute memorial to the courage and endurance of the garrison that fought behind those walls.

(Open at all times throughout the year.)

WINDSOR CASTLE

This is not only England's premier castle but, with its thirteen acres of precincts, the largest; it is also the largest inhabited castle in the world. It has the unique distinction of having been the principal home of English monarchs (apart from their London palaces) for 900 years, and is unique in other respects, too.

The first castle on this dominant site, overlooking the Thames as it laps round Windsor on its way east to London, was a timber fortress built by William the Conqueror immediately after his victory over Harold. A century later, timber was replaced by stone and, in the hands of successive kings—notably Henry I, II and III, and Edward III—it acquired the distinction it possesses today. Henry II built the magnificent keep, usually known as the Round Tower. It is an almost circular double shell, with an exterior diameter of about 100 ft, girdled by three baileys, the Lower, Middle and Upper Wards, in which the royal tournaments were held. Upper Ward has a so-called Norman gateway, actually constructed in the mid-fourteenth century when Edward III (who was born here) was doing so much to develop the castle as a whole. Inside the Round Tower there is a 165 ft well, over 6 ft in diameter and lined with stone for a third of its depth—a remarkable achievement for its period. Inside, too, are some timber buildings that date back no less than 600 years.

The Round Tower, however, is only one of the glories of the castle, though perhaps its chief one. There are the Henry III and Edward III Towers; there are the great walls erected by Henry I and III, and the Henry VIII gateway, flanked by huge polygonal towers; there is St George's Chapel, begun as long ago as 1475; there is the fourteenth-century Garter Chapter House (now part of the Deanery), and the unique Horseshoe Cloister; and there are the sumptuous State Apartments. But the catalogue is endless; only a tithe of Windsor Castle's glories have been touched upon. The whole great complex, with its towering walls, elaborated over the centuries, crowns this steep bluff that falls so sharply down to the water's edge as a jewel-studded crown might grace a royal brow. And from the turret above the Round House, when Her Majesty Queen Elizabeth II is in residence, flies her personal standard.

Open daily, all the year round. State Apartments only for certain hours, varying with the season and whether or not HM The Queen is in residence at the time.

Cornwall

LAUNCESTON CASTLE
(Off A30, near centre of the town)

Westward bound or eastward, to and from the West Country, you can easily miss the 'triple-crowned mounte' that 'retayneth the forme but not the fortune of former times', as a historian wrote of it in 1610—when the castle was already 300 years old. Why 'triple-crowned'? Because the periphery of the ancient motte is girdled by an earth wall partly reinforced with stone. Above this rises the outer wall of the thirteenth-century shell-keep, and inside, a near-unique feature, rises a two-storey cylindrical inner tower. These concentric structures constituting the keep are linked by a circular wall-walk that forms an unusually spacious platform for offensive defence. Viewed from the south, this keep, even though so much of its walls has disintegrated over the centuries, still presents an impressive appearance. It stands high on its motte in the north-east angle of the bailey (most of whose curtain walls have vanished) and is approached by a flight of stone steps between high walls, formerly roofed over as an added protection for its garrison.

Though so remote from the heart of England, seven centuries ago Launceston was the administrative centre of a vast earldom; it remained an assize town for 700 years, closely linked with its castle. The dyke which formerly protected its eastern wall has long since vanished, its ancient site being today's Castle Dyke Alley. From the town, you enter the castle by way of the South Gate, whose portcullis grooves may still be seen. On the opposite side of the bailey is the North Gate, again with portcullis grooves in evidence. More interesting, though, is the small room it contains, known as Doomsdale Tower: here George Fox, founder of the Society of Friends—the Quakers—was incarcerated in the seventeenth century. But, as always, it is the keep that dominates everything else. One of its interesting features, trivial perhaps but revealing, concerns the garderobe, or latrine, in the west wall. It was, of course, just a slit high on the outer side of the main wall but the designer of the castle took the trouble to arrange for a stone water-duct to 'flush' that section of the outer wall beneath it. So we have here at Launceston perhaps the earliest example of a lavatory cistern in English military architecture!

(Open during standard hours, see p 8, and also Sunday mornings, from April to September.)

Cornwall

PENDENNIS and ST MAWES CASTLES
(River Fal estuary)

These two coastal forts were built on the orders of Henry VIII and completed in 1543. They may be taken as a pair, for they are sited immediately opposite one another on the seaward side of Carrick Roads, a mile-wide stretch of water reaching deep inland from Falmouth Bay. Built high on a promontory, Pendennis commands the entrance from the west; St Mawes, built close to water level, was designed 'the better to annoy shipping'. Between them they defended the estuary from both east and west sides.

Built much later than the post-Norman castles, they incorporated cannon. The splay, both inwards and outwards, of the gun-ports that are a notable feature of Pendennis Castle made possible a wide, raking traverse of the water to south and to north. Close to the end of the promontory is the ditch and low sixteen-sided curtain wall enclosing a 35 ft high, circular three-storey tower, originally entered by a drawbridge over the ditch and protected by a portcullis that is still in position. Beyond this, inside the 16 ft walls, are three octagonal rooms, one above the other, in which arms and armour are displayed and you can inspect the mechanism for operating both drawbridge and portcullis. An internal spiral staircase gives access between basement kitchen and upper chambers. Pendennis Castle is pictured opposite.

Though it is sited on lower ground, St Mawes Castle is more elaborately laid out. It consists of a clover-leaf complex: a circular keep, approached by way of a drawbridge on the landward side and enclosed within three semicircular towers that reach to half its height. It is substantially taller than Pendennis, containing four floors, the uppermost of which is exactly 100 ft above sea level and carries a neat round watch-tower, of vital importance in those anxious days, four centuries ago, when invasion from the Continent was continuously expected. As at Pendennis, the kitchen occupied the basement deep down beneath the keep.

Both these castles ably fulfilled their functions until the mid-seventeenth century, when they were involved in the Civil War. Colonel 'Jack-for-the-King' Arundell defied the Parliamentary forces for five terrible months before surrendering Pendennis with honour, to march out 'with flying colours and trumpets sounding'. Strangely though, St Mawes capitulated at once, without the exchange of a single shot.

(Open during standard hours, see p 8, and also Sunday mornings, from April to September.)

RESTORMEL CASTLE
(Off B3268, 3 miles south of Bodmin)

This is a perfect example of a shell-keep perched on a motte given extra prominence by the digging of a circular ditch all round its base. The diameter of the curtain wall is 125 ft, the form is a perfect circle 8 ft thick and rising to more than 20 ft above the inner courtyard, while the slope of the motte falls steeply away from its foot in all directions. The whole dominates the west bank of the River Fowey, a mile or so above Lostwithiel. Built about 1100 AD by Baldwin Fitz Turstin, it commanded the bridge he threw across the river at the foot of the hill. Originally no more than a timber palisade, it was in due course replaced by stonework.

The earliest masonry is still discernible at the base of the gate tower, on the south-west curve; it was laid long before the curtain wall was built, for the castle gate was always its most vulnerable feature. During the twelfth century the noble circle of Cornish slate and Pentewan stone (from a quarry near by) was constructed; once this was complete, an inner concentric wall was built and the space between the two was successively filled with buildings. At courtyard level there were store-rooms and, at first-floor level, a succession of linked rooms: the great hall, the solar, the lord's bedchamber, the guest chamber. A kitchen filled the space between gate-house and great hall, with a serving-hatchway between them. Between the solar and main bedchamber was an ante-chapel which gave access to the chapel proper, the rectangular projection beyond the north-east curve of the wall, to which the priest's chamber was annexed. These buildings are largely thirteenth century in date, and the fact that the chapel was outside the curtain wall suggests that there was little fear of attack or siege. In fact, Restormel seems to have escaped involvement in fighting.

Nevertheless, it was prepared. You can see the grooves in the masonry of the gate tower in which the original drawbridge worked. Though water was brought in by a lead conduit from a spring on the west side, the castle had its own well, still to be seen but, curiously, nearer the chapel than the kitchen. Sets of steps, both of timber and of stone, gave access to the upper chambers and the top of the curtain wall; it is still possible to walk right round the castle behind its crenellations.

(Open during standard hours, see p 8, and also Sunday mornings, from April to September.)

Cornwall

TINTAGEL CASTLE
(Off B3263, 5 miles north-west of Camelford)

You should not approach this castle expecting to find a post-Norman building complete with keep and curtain walls, flanking towers and barbican and other traditional features. Tintagel stands in a class apart, primarily because of its astonishing situation; it is amazing that anything of it at all should have survived for over eight centuries in view of its site, subject to the fierceness of Atlantic weather. To reach it you must follow a track westwards to the tip of a promontory and thence climb to a near-island lying off its tip and almost completely surrounded by the restless sea. In remotest times this was the site of a small, courageous Celtic community of monks, as is revealed by the existence of some ancient rock-cut graves. These were partly destroyed when, in the first half of the twelfth century, Reginald, Earl of Cornwall and son of that great castle builder, Henry I, threw up the first walls, to tower above the sheer north-eastern face of those steep and treacherous cliffs.

The Upper and Lower Wards and Iron Gate are on the promontory itself, together with the remains of old buildings. A moment's glance at the conformation of the cliff shows why no flanking towers were built. From here, a further circuitous track brings you to the most ancient relics of Tintagel: the rectangular structure flanking the east side of the Inner Ward, which once contained the great hall and which is partly enclosed still by a thirteenth-century wall. Some ninety feet of the great hall structure, later adapted and elaborated, survive today, and reveal how splendid a creation it must have been, though now it is no more than a shell capable of inspiring speculation and wonder. It is not surprising, in view of the strength of the winds blowing off the Atlantic, that Tintagel should have fallen into such disrepair; it was too remote, also, for constant attention by those who maintained the castles on the mainland. It did, however, serve as a state prison in the fourteenth century: a prison site that matched Princetown on Dartmoor for bleakness and isolation.

The sheer romantic quality of the setting dominates every other aspect and accounts for the apparently unquenchable tradition that it was the Castle of King Arthur and the Knights of his Round Table. Alas, despite an alluring tradition, it was not!

(Open during standard hours, see p 8, and also Sunday mornings, from April to September.)

CARLISLE CASTLE

Carlisle was once a small, walled city on high ground just south of the River Eden; immediately to the north was the fiercely contested Scottish frontier. So it was a Border stronghold. For some five centuries it was the setting for almost continuous strife. Little of its walls remains, though entering from the south you will be confronted by a massive bastion of red sandstone. It is to the north of the city, between its main buildings and the meandering river, that the castle is to be found.

Though there was a stockade there soon after the Norman Conquest, the curtain walls and towers, gatehouses and keep, were not built until the middle of the twelfth century, when Henry I took it in hand. Today, those walls form a great triangle enclosing the outer bailey, or Castle Green and, in the eastern angle, a triangular inner ward overlooked by the keep, the whole complex yet further protected by an inner curtain wall. Secure on an eminence, protected by moat and earthworks, it is not surprising that the castle withstood attack and siege time and again throughout the five centuries of its active life, that virtually ended with the '45 Rebellion.

Thanks to the warm colour of its locally quarried stone, the walls, towers and keep are less forbidding than many others, but they match them in design and construction. In these more peaceful days they form an appropriate HQ for the 2nd Battalion, the Border Regiment, housing one of the finest military museums in the country, well worth visiting quite apart from the major interest of the castle itself.

There is plenty to see here, both on the heroic, historic scale and in smaller detail. The Captain's Tower, for instance; Queen Mary's Tower (Mary Queen of Scots was Elizabeth's prisoner here in 1568); and, as always, the keep. This is more than 60 ft high and square, its 12 ft thick walls massively buttressed. Within embrasures are innumerable incised memorials, 'picture writing' of prisoners incarcerated here over the centuries, whether civil (such as poachers in royal preserves) or military. You will admire the great scope and elaboration of the buildings; but you will perhaps carry away with you, among your strongest memories, these mute reminders of men who lingered within these walls and suffered and eventually died there.

(Open during standard hours, see p 8, and also Sunday mornings, from April to September.)

Derbyshire

PEVERIL CASTLE
(At Castleton, on A625, 16 miles west of Sheffield)

It is small wonder that Scott refers to this as being 'built upon principles on which the eagle selects her eyrie'. The road through Castleton in the Hope Valley, runs almost 400 ft sheer beneath the hill immediately to the south of the village on which, at a height of 1,000 ft, the castle stands, its walls almost overhanging the precipitous northern face. Beneath the west flank is the ravine, Cave Dale, entrance to Peak Cavern; beyond is Mam Tor, the 'Shivering Mountain'.

Peveril, or Peak, Castle was built soon after the Conquest and given to William Peverel, natural son of William the Conqueror. A triangle of curtain walls outlines the summit of the hill, the northern section being the most substantial, and so the best preserved, because the rocky summit sloped in that direction. Because there was so much good stone available it was used, rather than timber, from the first. But though the site was so formidable, the castle was continuously strengthened throughout succeeding centuries. The great keep in the south-west angle was built in 1176; 40 ft square, it still stands to almost its original height. Its outer walls rise above the roof, enclosing a rain-water trough from which the chute can still be seen. As usual, the main chamber is to be found on the first floor.

In the courtyard are the remains of the enclosed buildings: the old and the new great halls of the eleventh and thirteenth centuries. Henry II stayed here in the twelfth century, Edward III in the fourteenth. Internal strife tended to bypass Peveril—the terrain and weather were perhaps too challenging—so it lost its importance as a factor in warfare. Experts maintain that its chief function was to protect the valuable lead mines of the district. It offers scope for detective work in other fields, too. The eastern round tower contains building material that no one could make in Britain at the time it was built. Close examination has revealed that this material came from neighbouring Brough, a Roman fortress two miles down the valley once known as Anavio. The Romans made the bricks, like thick red tiles, that are to be seen in so many of their buildings; and Brough, it seems, was 'cannibalised' in the thirteenth century by the tower builders.

(Open during standard hours, see p 8, and also Sunday mornings, from April to September.)

Devonshire

DARTMOUTH CASTLE
(On west side of the Dart estuary, 1 mile south-east of Dartmouth)

Five hundred years ago Dartmouth was a merchants' stronghold and base, flourishing and progressive, its roadstead an anchorage for countless vessels. For long it had been the chief port for the Bordeaux wine merchants; it had furnished ships and men for the siege of Calais; its importance and wealth were recognised, and were also a cause of envy, so that it needed to be safeguarded from attacks by its many rivals. Hence the construction of the castle, in the late fifteenth century, designed to be both offensive and defensive: it was the first castle built in England that incorporated the requirements of artillery manned by the garrison behind the walls.

It is unusual in design: a massive round tower somewhat awkwardly combined with a square tower, both rising three storeys. In the seaward walls are square-cut gun-ports, so fashioned that the guns within could be swivelled to produce a raking crossfire commanding the whole extent of the seaward mouth of the estuary. Nor was this all. The earliest defence mechanism was a chain of massive links suspended beneath the surface of the water between the base of the castle and the masonry of Gomerock, on the east bank. At need, this chain could be pulled taut by the manipulation of a sturdy double winch set low in the tower and turned by man-power so that it stretched across at water level, a reliable trap and barricade against intrusive vessels, whether from Brittany or further afield. The grooves for the winch axles may still be seen in the stonework. Edward VI contributed annually to the maintenance of the chain.

You will find such features as gun-platforms absent from post-Norman castles, but present here at Dartmouth, where they were successively elaborated, as during the Civil War, for instance, when the Royalist garrison eventually surrendered. Again at the time of the Napoleonic Wars too, when the castle was a gathering-point for volunteers, and later in the same century when there was another threat of invasion from France. And yet again as recently as 1940, when the Old Battery was equipped with 4.7 ordnance, to be used in the event of a yet greater invasion—which did not materialise. Seen from the water, the castle is immensely forbidding; from within, there is a superb view eastwards. It contains a minor museum of local military history.

(Open during standard hours, see p 8, and also Sunday mornings, from April to September.)

COLCHESTER CASTLE

Roman Camulodunum was an important town a thousand years before the Normans came to it; its massive Roman-built walls had been repaired only a century before. The Normans reversed the process, however, 'cannibalising' the Temple of Claudius and much else for the Roman brickwork to augment the local stone and stone from Caen, which they used to build on the Roman site the castle whose remains even today lie within the heart of the town, only yards away from the bypass that skirts it to the north. Near the East Anglian coast and Thames estuary, this site has always been one of significance.

A Norman outer ditch, and stone-reinforced earthworks partially encircle the inner bailey to north and east; within stands the keep. Though it no longer rises to its original height of 90 ft, with flanking towers topping the hundred, it is still reputedly the largest rectangular keep in the country, possibly designed by the architect of London's White Tower, which is in fact smaller. It was entered by a highly elaborate and ingenious approach-route whose three right-angle bends were designed to frustrate the enemy; its walls are over 12 ft thick and stand on foundations 17 ft thick that penetrate some 25 ft into the ground. All the masonry is of special interest, not least for the elaborate herringbone work that incorporates Roman brick and tile with the Kentish ragstone and finer Normandy stone from Caen.

The interior of the keep is rich in interest. It possesses the largest known newel staircase, in the south-west tower; the garderobe in the north-west tower is particularly well preserved. Because the castle has been used as a prison for six centuries at least, it has an incomparable display of prisoners' carvings on the inner walls. Here, in the notorious 'Oven', eighteen-year-old James Parnell, the first Quaker martyr, languished in the vilest conditions, to die of his sufferings. Here countless men and women were tortured before being burned to death for heresy or for other crimes punishable in harsher days by death. Strangely, though, just three centuries ago the castle was privately sold for demolition, but not so surprisingly, its massive walls resisted. In recompense, perhaps, it was to some extent restored, and is now a fine, impressive example of an ancient monument cherished and preserved.

(Open on weekdays throughout the year, from 10 to 5, except for Good Friday, Christmas Day and Boxing Day. Also between April and September, it is open on Sundays from 2.30 to 5.)

Essex

HEDINGHAM CASTLE
(Off A604, 4 miles north-east of Halstead)

Of the original castle, built in the late eleventh and early twelfth centuries, only the giant keep still stands. Poised magnificently on a natural eminence of rock, and still partly surrounded by the moat its builders added to strengthen the site, it is one of the oldest, grandest and starkest of the great post-Norman rectangular keeps. It rises 100 ft into the air, with two of its original four corner turrets still standing; its 60 ft walls are 12 ft thick at the base, and still 10 ft thick at the top, where they enclose the fifth storey. The other castle buildings were destroyed in the course of sieges up to four centuries after they were erected, but the towering keep seems all the more impressive today for the sense of grim isolation it communicates to the wondering visitor; its gaunt, uncompromising, sheer cold stone walls still have the power to offer challenge with a hint of menace implicit.

Originally, the usual fore-building with drawbridge and portcullis that could be operated by the garrison, protected the entrance. Today that has gone, and you enter at first-floor level by way of a massive four-arched bridge constructed of Tudor bricks whose warmth contrasts strongly with the grey stone of the high walls beyond. You find yourself in the main strongroom, where the garrison massed for defence or sortie while the lord's family and non-fighting retainers anxiously waited above, this keep being at once a stronghold and a residence. A stone spiral stairway leads to the upper chambers, and you will notice that it turns clockwise. This was deliberate for it gave the retreating defender the advantage over the invader as his own sword-arm was free while the other's was cramped against the newel as he fought his way upwards. Above is the banqueting hall, and above that the gallery and sleeping-quarters, some of them alcoves cut out of the very thickness of the walls.

Hedingham's history is inseparable from that of the great and ancient family of the de Veres. Its fortunes and theirs rose and fell together, and they held it, on and off, until 1625. One of them became Constable of the Tower of London; another entertained Queen Elizabeth I; yet another became Lord Great Chamberlain. Their superb keep, gaunt on its hilltop, is their lasting and very impressive memorial.

(Open Easter Monday; then May-September on Tuesdays, Thursdays and Saturdays from 2-6; on Whit-Monday and August Bank Holiday from 10-6.)

Gloucestershire

BERKELEY CASTLE
(Off A38, 18 miles north of Bristol)

Berkeley claims to be the oldest inhabited castle in the country. It has been occupied by one family—dynasty might be the more appropriate word—for over eight centuries. It stands on an eminence overlooking the River Severn with the Welsh Marches beyond. Before the Conquest, there was a fortified manor on the site, owned by Earl Godwin, King Harold's father; after the Battle of Hastings, William the Conqueror gave orders for it to be converted into a true Border castle.

In the next century Henry II gave it to Robert FitzHarding, ancestor of the Berkeleys; and it was his son who built the enormous curtain walls and massive keep. This is unusual in that, instead of being perched on top of the motte (artificial or natural) on which the Normans built their keeps, it was made large enough to enclose the motte entirely; it is of the type known as a shell-keep. You enter it through a fourteenth-century arched doorway inset within the original twelfth-century one, an arch that is still visible around it. Once inside, history—and grim history at that—makes an immediate impact upon you. Here, some six centuries ago, the unhappy King Edward II was imprisoned; here he was eventually done to death.

In a corner of the keep, ironically known as the King's Gallery, there may be seen what appears to be a well, but in fact it is the entrance to a 30 ft deep dungeon. Rotting carcasses of cattle, and sometimes living prisoners too, used to be thrown into it and the stench of putrefying flesh rose strongly enough to kill off any unlucky prisoner in the chamber. Edward II did not die in that barbarous fashion but was brutally murdered by his gaolers, Sir John Maltravers and Sir Thomas Gurney.

The exterior of the castle—ramparts, turrets, curtain walls, gateways and battlements—is less grim. This is partly because much of the outer stonework possesses a delicate 'rose-petal-pink' hue. The stone came from quarries on the bank of the Severn, which flows past the castle to the west. It contrasts strongly, therefore, with the stark white of, say, Dover and Arundel, or the menacing dark of Alnwick. Its apparent softness enables one to forget the horrors of the dungeon set beneath the sinister keep that dominates the whole complex from almost every direction.

(Open April 1 - September 30 daily, except Mondays, from 2-5.30; Bank Holiday Mondays from 11-5.30; Sundays only in October from 2-4.30.)

32

Hampshire (Isle of Wight)

CARISBROOKE CASTLE
(2 miles south-west of Newport)

This splendid castle stands almost at the dead centre of the island. It is note-worthy not only for the condition of its walls and five immense bastions jutting out to the main compass-points, with an extra one flanking the west gateway, but also for the fact that so many 'layers' of history are simultaneously in evidence. Roman stonework protrudes beneath the Norman earthworks; an eleventh-century motte dominates the 150 ft square inner bailey; a twelfth-century shell-keep looms over the motte, accessible by a flight of sixty or more stone steps; two fine fourteenth-century drum-towers brace the gateway. There are fifteenth-century doors, and sixteenth-century rampart-walks and artillery bases, constructed on the orders of Elizabeth I herself. It is rare to see so many strata of history so notably displayed within one complex of military building; here you almost literally turn the pages of history.

The inner, or West, Bailey opens outwards into the East Bailey, and the whole complex lies within fine earthworks edged with stone. From the air the layout is an ornate geometric pattern, much more emphatic than many ancient castles that seem to merge into the landscape from which they spring. And it is in the West Bailey that most features of greatest interest are located, small as well as large.

There are the triple portcullis grooves in the gate; the domestic chambers in the former great hall in which, for nearly a year, Charles I was incarcerated and from which he made an abortive attempt to escape; the Leper Squint in the south wall of St Peter's Chapel; the well in the south-east corner with the ancient tread-wheel operated by a donkey, or sometimes by a pair of prisoners. And in the north-east corner the polygonal shell-keep with its own 160 ft well sunk unhygienically close to the garderobes set as usual, like the great fire-places, in the exterior curtain wall.

For many centuries the buildings in the West Bailey were the residence, first of the lords, then of the captains and, for four centuries past, of the governors of the island, an office currently held by Earl Mountbatten of Burma. Part, however, is now a museum. So here, in essence, is a museum of historical masonry, within which the visitor can study the artefacts and memorials of those who occupied both the island and the castle itself.

(Open during standard hours, see p 8, throughout the year.)

34

PORTCHESTER CASTLE
(Off A27, 5 miles north of Portsmouth)

This, as the name indicates, was a Roman 'castrum' overlooking a harbour. Seventeen centuries ago the Romans added to the 'Saxon shore defences' of Reculver, Pevensey and Richborough this magnificent specimen, the only Roman fortress in northern Europe whose walls remain wholly intact. They cover nine acres: a square with rule-straight sides 200 yards long, the eastern and southern walls washed by the waters of the harbour to which access was available by the Water Gate on the east side.

The Romans abandoned the site and for six centuries it was deserted until, in the early twelfth century, an Augustinian Priory was established in the south-eastern corner of the square and, at the same time, the splendid medieval fortress, started by Henry I and developed by successive monarchs, was sited in the diametrically opposite corner. There the enormous keep dominates the whole site and harbour to this day. For more than three centuries this fort was elaborated and strengthened. The great curtain walls went up; the keep, with 8 ft thick walls (13 ft at the base) enclosing a 40 ft square space, massively buttressed, served many purposes, including a King's Treasury and a state prison. Indeed, as close scrutiny will show you, it has housed prisoners for many centuries; you may read the scrawled signatures of soldiers captured during the Napoleonic Wars in their hundreds and incarcerated here. They add a personal, intimate note to the tale of international strife.

A moat encloses the two sides of the inner bailey not protected by the north and west walls, its inner bank buttressing them and the corner tower, at their foot. Inside those walls are the remains of the buildings successively established there: the palace of Richard II, and the great hall and adjacent kitchen and servery abutting against the massive gatehouse on the south side of the bailey. From this a bridge gave access across the moat to the outer bailey and so to the Water Gate and the Land Gate which still occupy the sites carved for them in the walls by the Romans. Through the Land Gate marched the expeditionary force that triumphed at Agincourt in 1415; from the Water Gate they sailed when 'fair stood the wind for France'.

(Open during standard hours, see p 8, and also Sunday mornings, from April to September.)

GOODRICH CASTLE
(Off A40, 4 miles south of Ross-on-Wye)

Finely sited on a spur of rock high above the right bank of the River Wye, overlooking a once vital ford close to the Symonds Yat loop, this castle was first built some time in the eleventh century by Godrick Mappestone, whose name it bears though it was largely rebuilt in the following century; only a fragment here and there of the original remains. The curtain walls date from about 1300. With their three corner-bastions and a gatehouse on the north-east corner approached by a finely preserved barbican, they enclose a bailey containing a twelfth-century square keep, great hall, solar, chapel tower, kitchen and other buildings. Goodrich was compact, well planned and organised, a sufficient stronghold.

Look where you will, there is always something of interest. The three-storey keep, the oldest surviving portion, is flanked by the grimmest of dungeons, well below rock level. The fine south-east, south-west and north-west towers, though cylindrical for most of their height, spring from beautifully proportioned square spur-plinths. The whole south wall of the kitchen is occupied by a great fireplace with flanking ovens; the 65 ft long great hall fills most of the west side of the bailey. But probably the most striking feature of the whole complex of masonry is, for once, the barbican. Situated outside the north-east corner of the bailey, it consists of a semi-circular thirteenth-century 10 ft wall pierced by a bridge (formerly a drawbridge) between towers and leading to a second bridge at right-angles to its line (again originally a drawbridge, the sockets in which it pivoted being still in evidence) which gives access to the gatehouse and bailey beyond. This was a not unusual device, calculated to slow down the progress of invaders anticipating no more than one substantial obstacle in their path.

Close to the turbulent Welsh Border, Goodrich was constantly involved in fighting. But until the sixteenth century it was also the seat of generations of Earls of Shrewsbury. Inevitably it had to play its part in the Civil War, a pawn in the dispute between Royalists and Parliamentarians. Its days were numbered, and with the surrender of Charles in 1646, it too surrendered. As usual, there came about the regulation 'slighting' of this noble castle by the Parliamentarians. So, after the vicissitudes of five centuries the long years of its glory came to an end.

(Open during standard hours, see p 8, and also Sunday mornings, from April to September.)

DEAL CASTLE

(On the coast, midway between Sandown and Walmer Castles)

This is the middle one of 'The Three Castles which keep the Downs'—the Downs being the important anchorage between the coast and the Goodwin Sands four miles to the east. This stretch of coastline, from Julius Caesar's day onwards, has been an obvious point of invasion from the Continent. Anticipating such an invasion, Henry VIII set a vast body of men to work, and this most original and beautifully designed castle was completed in 1540. Seen from the air, it is a six-petalled 'flower' complete with six inner 'sepals' enclosing the central 'bud', the keep. There is no other castle in all England that presents a more perfectly symmetrical pattern.

Approach from the landward side (it stands literally on the sea edge) by way of a stone ramp linking the outer earthworks with the outer semicircular bastions, involves crossing two concentric dry moats, each powerfully defended by ordnance that could fire on the intruding enemy from both sides. The ordnance included 32-pounders, 18-pounders and 6-pounders as well as arquebus; the larger cannon could command the full width of the Downs, so that no approach by sea was practicable until the guns had been silenced from the land —a hopeless task.

Within the ingeniously contrived outer fortifications may be found an elaborate system of linked guardrooms, store-rooms, armoury and gun-emplacements. As always, the keep would be the final refuge, but here it was so amply defended in advance that it was impregnable. A drawbridge (now replaced); portcullis, with 'murder-holes' for the vertical discharge of missiles; zigzag corridors and offset gates, interior ordnance covering all of them; a trapdoor in the gatehouse floor leading down to a dungeon: these were but a few of the devices incorporated here for the repulse of the invader. Not surprisingly, Deal Castle remained inviolate until the Civil War. Eventually it capitulated to the overwhelming strength of the Royalists, though not until its mighty neighbour, Walmer, had surrendered. In the next century the Royal Navy took over the duties for which these three Downs castles were originally built and garrisoned; Governors' Lodgings were built on the seaward side—a sign that a period of peace was now officially anticipated on this south-eastern coastline.

(Open during standard hours, see p 8, and also Sunday mornings, from April to September.)

DOVER CASTLE

There is no more impressive castle site in all England than Castle Hill; and no site is more gloriously crowned than this on which Dover Castle was built. Here, some three thousand years ago, iron-age man threw up the first earthworks for his safety. Two thousand years ago the Romans erected on it a lighthouse whose massive remains still stand within the ramparts. Here, nine centuries ago, Harold of England surrendered the existing castle to William the Conqueror. 'The Key of England', it has been called; for 900 years and more, men have looked out over its battlements across the twenty-one miles of English Channel which separate Dover from Calais.

What confronts you today, as you climb towards that tremendous array of curtain walls and mural towers, gateways and battlements, barbican, bailey and tower keep, is the result of many centuries of refortification, strengthening, and elaboration of the original structure, to keep pace with developments in weapons and defensive techniques, most notably in the twelfth and thirteenth centuries. Henry II was responsible for the most outstanding individual feature: the great tower which dominates the inner bailey, the oldest part of the castle. Almost 100 ft high and square, with 20 ft thick walls, it is one of the noblest of all our rectangular keeps.

A century later, under Henry III, the magnificent Constable's Gate was built on the western side of the array of ramparts, walls and towers: a splendidly proportioned arched gateway flanked by massive drum-towers forming a barbican to protect it. The Constable was Governor, or Warden. The first constable was William I's half-brother, Odo of Bayeux; four centuries later the Duke of York, later to be enthroned as Henry VIII, held the office; four centuries later still it was the Duke of Wellington; and, a hundred years after him, Sir Winston Churchill.

The towers and gates are evocatively named: Crevecoeur, Avranche, Godsfoe; Penchester, Rokesley, St John, and a score more, evidence of Norman and English rivalry and domination. Indeed, nine centuries of vivid history lie embedded within these great walls and towers, this array of gleaming stone and flint rising so spectacularly from a green turf hill first exploited and built upon nearly thirty centuries ago.

(Open during standard hours, see p 8, and also Sunday mornings, from April to September.)

ROCHESTER CASTLE

(On A2, 30 miles east of London)

William the Conqueror ordered the building of this castle which stands on a dominating site above the River Medway. Three sides were flanked by a moat, and the whole enclosed by massive walls 300 ft long and 20 ft high. Though there are remnants of these today, the great rectangular keep ranks with the finest in the country; its 12 ft thick walls are 70 ft long and rise well above 100 ft, with a turret at each angle, that at the south corner being a thirteenth-century replacement of the original one, and rounded in form. It may strike the visitor as strange that the first castle was built by a Norman monk, and the eventual triumphant achievement of the keep executed by a twelfth-century archbishop of Canterbury. But it must be remembered that the monks built many of our finest surviving medieval priories, monasteries, abbeys and bridges; they built, as always, to last.

And, as always, the keep today is the outstanding focal point of interest. It is entered by way of the traditional fore-building, at the east corner, from which a bridge spans the dungeon. A spiral staircase near by climbs to the lofty summit. The centre of the keep is divided by a notable arcaded partition-wall which contains a striking feature: a central well that served not only the basement but every floor of the keep. Its depth, they will tell you there, varies with the local tides.

Before you start the long climb to the top, look for the portcullis grooves by the first-floor gate, and also for that odd recess designed to take the porter's keys and lantern. Thence to the original and essential chapel, and so to the great hall, an astonishing chamber whose roof is more than 30 ft high, supported on great columns linked by arches. Above this is another storey containing a chamber surrounded by mural galleries set against the enormously thick walls.

The great siege of Rochester Castle was in 1215 when King John was present in person and its hard-pressed garrison were reduced to eating their horses before eventual capitulation. Later, it withstood Simon de Montfort. Then it fell into disrepair, but happily this was checked and, thanks to the far-sightedness of the authorities, it survives to this day as a magnificent example of Norman castle building.

(Open during standard hours, see p 8, and also Sunday mornings, from April to September.)

WALMER CASTLE
(Off A258, 2 miles south of Deal)

Since the beginning of the eighteenth century this has been, and still remains, the official residence of the Lords Warden of the Cinque Ports, in which glowing record two names stand out pre-eminently: the Duke of Wellington and Sir Winston Churchill. But this is not to suggest that the castle is relatively new. In fact, with Deal and Sandown a few miles to the north, this was one of 'The Three Castles which keep the Downs', the anchorage between the coastline and the dangerous Goodwin Sands, and was built by Henry VIII in 1539 as a safeguard against threatened invasion from the other side of the Channel. Like Deal, Walmer is beautifully symmetrical in plan. Four semicircular bastion towers, linked by short, thick, curved walls, make up the curtain embracing a central, circular tower which forms the 'core'; the pattern is almost exaggeratedly compact, close-knit. From the centre rose a circular keep, separated from the tower-flanked curtain wall by a narrow, sheltered courtyard that gave access between keep and curtain walls and towers, and the gunports pierced in them all round. In addition there was a continuous, protected gallery right round the inner side of the walls, and added protection was afforded by guns mounted high in the keep itself.

As the years became more peaceful and the castle was required more for residential than defensive purposes, alterations came about. One bastion tower was heightened less than a century ago; the drawbridge over the moat was replaced by an ordinary bridge by which you enter today. But overhead, still visible, are the eight 'murder-holes' through which missiles and burning oil could be dropped on the heads of would-be invaders temporarily halted by the formidable portcullis. On entering, you find yourself on the ground floor which housed the main armoury and ammunition for the cannon, notably the 32-pound muzzle-loaders which were fired from the gun-ports on the seaward side. Specimens of these are still on view, a tacit but clear-cut reminder of the offensive strength of this coastal fort in days gone by. On the upper floor are the rooms occupied by the governor, or constable; and later, when invasion ceased to threaten, by the long succession of distinguished Lords Warden, many of whose personal possessions are on show here as reminders of their residency.

(Open during standard hours, see p 8, and also Sunday mornings, from April to September. Closed when the Lord Warden is in residence, usually in August.)

Lancashire

LANCASTER CASTLE

Though it seems a paradox, this castle is both ancient and relatively new. As its name suggests, it is basically a Roman fortress, a 'castrum' erected by Agricola eighteen centuries ago overlooking the navigable, and therefore potentially dangerous, Lune River. Evidence of its Roman origin exists in the name of one of its great towers, Hadrian's Tower, which has Roman masonry in its lowest courses, but not in the late-fourteenth-early-fifteenth-century gateway, John O'Gaunt's Tower, which has a statue of the man, 'Time-honoured Lancaster', in a niche (to remind one that the castle was a gift from King Henry). This, though, is only one of a number of noble towers forming a castle started by Roger of Poitou in the eleventh century. There is the Norman keep, or Lungess Tower, 70 ft high and 80 ft square. Above it is a turret, John O'Gaunt's Chair, formerly a lookout post with a view as far as the Isle of Man, and also the frame for the beacon-fire lit to give warning of invaders along the coast. Innumerable prisoners were held here, among them so many Quakers (including George Fox, founder of the Society of Friends) that a chamber high up in the keep is named after them. But there are grimmer types of 'security' to be found here. It has been a major prison for 900 years and remains so still. You pass through 9 ft thick walls and iron-studded oak doors to enter the dank, virtually unventilated dungeons, some of which were only discovered in comparatively recent times. These are the punishment cells; the branding-iron and other instruments of torture are there to be seen. Near by is the Drop Room where condemned prisoners were manacled before being led to Hanging Corner, where little more than a century ago, prisoners were still publicly hanged in full view of the church opposite.

Not all of the castle is open to the public, but the wall-walk and roof-walk give a clear impression of how an ancient castle was ruthlessly 'slighted' at the end of the Civil War as a punishment for its sturdy resistance to the Parliamentarians. In succeeding centuries it was skilfully and intelligently rehabilitated to re-establish it as today's Shire Hall and Assize Court (or Crown Court) within containing-walls that are an impressive reminder of the history it has witnessed.

(Open for officially conducted tours only. Easter weekend, except Sunday, in the morning and afternoon; between Easter and Whitsun, in the morning and afternoon, but Wednesdays and Saturdays in the afternoon only; after Whitsun, daily in the mornings and afternoons. Earliest conducted tour is at 10.30; last tour is at 4. Additional conducted tours can be arranged.)

LINCOLN CASTLE

The castle was built immediately after the Conquest, and on a site largely within the walls of the old Roman fort on Ermine Street. With the Minster to the east, it occupies the high ground dominating the city to the north. It spreads over more than six acres, and its former moats and ramparts, beyond the curtain wall, more than doubled this considerable area. The entrance to the great oval bailey is on the eastern, or Minster, side; a well-proportioned pointed arch rises in front of the original Norman rounded arch and the angles are capped by turrets containing the remains of the spiral stairs. On the far side of the bailey is the western gateway, no longer in use but interesting because it has not been altered from its original design and the portcullis grooves can still be seen. There are two great mounds, some two hundred feet apart, within the bailey. On the westernmost stands the keep, also known as the Lucy Tower after the wife of one of the earliest sheriffs of Lincolnshire and keeper of the king's most important castle in the county, who almost certainly built it. It is a notable example of a shell-keep, open to the sky and curious in the fact that externally it has fifteen sides while inside it has no more than twelve.

Within the curtain walls are other buildings of considerable interest. At the north-east corner is the horseshoe-shaped Cobb Hall, containing many inscriptions by prisoners immured within its walls who later died on the gallows which, until little more than a century ago, stood on its roof. In the south-east corner of the bailey, built on a 40 ft mound, is the Observatory Tower, a post-Norman structure to which additions were made in the fourteenth century and a turret was added in the nineteenth century by a governor of Lincoln gaol (then inside the castle) with a keen interest in astronomy. The prison buildings were, and remain, close alongside.

The castle was from the first involved in strife. Matilda seized it from King Stephen in 1140, and it changed hands over and again. During the Civil War it was held in turn by the Parliamentarians and by the Royalists, but eventually capitulated to the Parliamentarians in 1644. Militarily speaking, its career ended there, but it continued to be the county gaol, and to this day contains the Courts of Assize.

(Open on weekdays from April to September between 10 and 6; from October to March between 10 and 4. Also, from May to September on Sundays between 2 and 7.30; and in April and October on Sundays between 2 and 5.)

Lincolnshire

TATTERSHALL CASTLE
(On A153, 15 miles south-east of Lincoln)

Though Tattershall does not lie on any strategic route there was a modest castle here in the early thirteenth century. What you see today, possibly the most impressive fifteenth-century brick-built edifice in all England, is the great tower of a castle-mansion built by Ralph, third Baron Cromwell. He had fought at Agincourt, survived, and been appointed Lord Treasurer of England. This was a post that inevitably meant hostility from those whom he could force to pay monetary tribute to the throne; thus, though the mansion he constructed for himself was to be lavishly appointed, it had at the same time to be capable of defence. Today, virtually all that remains is the superb tower. It and the inner bailey are encircled by a moat, and this in turn is encircled by an outer moat. To obtain his objective, an enemy had to negotiate an elaborate system of drawbridges protected by guardhouses distributed about the outer and middle wards and capable of sustained defence. The remains of these guardhouses are still to be seen as you make your way towards the tower.

The tower entirely dominates the flat Lincolnshire landscape. It stands four storeys high, rectangular, with sides 87 ft by 67 ft and more than 20 ft thick. Two fine octagonal corner-towers flank its western face, rising high above the main walls, with machicolated parapets higher even than the machicolations of the walls, designed to enable defenders to drop missiles on invaders struggling at their foot.

The colour of its 322,000 bricks glows warmly over a cold landscape, almost incandescent in rich morning or evening sunlight. The many windows, too, emphasise the point that pure defence was less important to the designer than the splendour and amenities appropriate to a privately occupied mansion— even though, essentially, a fortified one. Inside the tower are the lord's chambers, one above the other, still impressive in their size and distinctive features. Today, the houses, farms and other buildings composing the hamlet, named after a succession of thirteenth-century Robert Tateshales, encroach upon the site. But the lines of the concentric moats enclosing the three spacious wards can still be traced, spreading eastwards and northwards from the glory of the great tower itself.

(Open all the year: weekdays from 9.30-7; Sundays 1-7 or dusk if earlier.)

52

THE TOWER OF LONDON

There is more history to the square yard here than is to be found anywhere else in England: a record covering almost twenty centuries. William of Normandy built the castle within city walls laid out a thousand years earlier by the Romans and rebuilt centuries later by King Alfred. Soon the castle was enlarged eastwards, but the Roman relics are still to be seen. This twenty-acre site, washed on the south side by the Thames, was originally surrounded by a moat that enclosed the outer curtain wall; within lay the outer ward, girdled by an inner curtain wall flanked by thirteen bastion towers that enclosed the inner ward, with its various buildings set against the inner side of the walls. From the centre there soars the magnificent 90 ft keep, or White Tower, with walls more than 100 ft long and 15 ft thick, one of the earliest and largest keeps in all Europe. It is a landmark for miles in most directions.

The Tower of London has been both palace and castle for many centuries. Within the keep or the surrounding towers—Bell and Byward, Beauchamp and Bloody, Martin, Salt and Wakefield and others—have languished kings and queens, assassins and innocents through ten eventful centuries. Here Lady Jane Grey was executed; here Guy Fawkes and his fellow conspirators were first tried; through the well-named Traitor's Gate, beneath St Thomas' Tower on Thames-side, passed Henry VIII's second and fifth wives, Anne Boleyn and Katharine Howard, on their way to prison and execution, as did the Earl of Essex and the Dukes of Monmouth and Buckingham and countless other nobles fallen into disgrace; the scaffold and block were situated within the inner ward.

There is more to see here than in perhaps any dozen other castles combined. The various Armouries; the Sword Room and Weapon Room; the Tudor Room and Bloody Tower; the Martin Tower, scene of Colonel Blood's attempt, just three centuries ago, to steal the Crown Jewels; the staircase site beneath the Great Tower where, some three hundred years ago, children's bones identified as those of Edward V and his young brother were unearthed, partly solving a mystery that dated back to the time of Richard III. Yet so rich in record is the Tower of London that in these paragraphs only a microscopic fraction of its story has even been touched upon.

(Open daily throughout the year: mid-March to end of April from 10-4.30; May to September from 10 to 5; October to mid-March from 10-4. Also on Sundays, mid-March to late October from 2-5.)

54

GROSMONT CASTLE

(Off B4347, 10 miles north-east of Abergavenny)

With Skenfrith and Llantilio near by, this makes up the trio of early thirteenth-century castles built in the ancient Manor of Upper Gwent: small but highly effective Norman strongholds in the border country, an area which they had seized from the Welsh. They replaced the earlier Norman strongholds which were nothing more than timber buildings enclosed within massive timber palisades and a moat, possibly fed by the neighbouring River Monnow. Grosmont in particular reveals three successive building periods in these so-called 'trilaterals': two in the early thirteenth century and the third in the early fourteenth century—a feature that is not unusual among castles.

The earliest remains consist of the huge rectangular block on the east side of the inner bailey, nearly 100 ft long and a third as wide, buttressed at the corners. Its ground floor would have been the usual store-rooms and kitchen; above were the great hall and the lord's private apartments, with windows over-looking the surrounding moat on three sides and the bailey on the fourth. The bailey itself is enclosed by a fine curtain wall in three equal straight lengths with drum-towers at the angles, and closed at the south-western end by the gatehouse which adjoins the angle of the great hall. The gatehouse is impressive: a vaulted entrance passage over 40 ft long and proportionately wide, with a two-storey building over it and side walls projecting outwards to flank the pit that contained the balance-weight for the original drawbridge—a minor barbican, in fact. Gatehouse, curtain walls and drum-towers are all rather later than the great hall block, and the whole assembly is massed on an artificially raised earth and stone platform above the surrounding ground level and moat which is curved round the wall, but runs straight on the east side.

There were further additions in the early fourteenth century, less impressive than the main block, curtain walls and towers, one of which rises through no fewer than four storeys. For a while this was a royal castle, in the hands of Henry III, Prince Edward and, later, Edmund 'Crouchback', Earl of Lancaster. Probably its most dramatic period was during the long siege by Owen Glendower, in 1405, when its sorely tried garrison was eventually relieved by Prince Henry himself.

(Open during standard hours, see p 8, throughout the year.)

MONMOUTH CASTLE

The site has been utilised by castle builders since pre-Roman times: a high plateau partly encircled to south, west and north by the River Monnow and on the east by the Wye, of which the Monnow is a tributary. The famous gate tower on the Monnow bridge is an outpost. The sprawling town climbs westwards up the slope, its Castle Street ending at the original gateway to the oval bailey, which is ringed on three sides by the rock and turf rampart falling steeply to the river, and on the townward side, originally at least, by an artificial ditch spanned by a bridge close beneath the gateway.

Immediately inside Castle Ward you are confronted by the remains of the Norman castle towering on the far west side, sheer above the curving line of the river. William Fitz Osbern of Breteuil, who fought at Hastings, built this castle and others in the last years before his death in 1071. For many years it remained the administrative centre of this important Marcher Lordship in the contested borderland; it was here that, in 1387, the future King Henry V was born.

It was inevitably involved mainly in local skirmishes, for the Welsh and English were never easy neighbours. It was a Royalist stronghold in the Civil War, capitulating at last before insuperable odds; thereafter, as always, it suffered the virtually irreparable indignity of 'slighting' at the Parliamentarians' hands. The famous Round Tower, on whose foundations Great Castle House was soon afterwards erected, was completely destroyed; the gateway too. But the keep, or great tower, dating from the early twelfth century, and the adjacent great hall, built a century or so later, were not so completely destroyed. Though much of the west wall of the keep has now collapsed, sufficient of its other walls remains to show how fine a building it was. So, too, the remains of the great hall, the 'Steward's Hall Beside the Great Tower', over 60 ft long and over 30 ft wide. Long after the 'slighting' of the castle it remained in use as Monmouth's Assize Court. Today the town sleeps on the fringe of the bailey, separated by Monnow Street and Agincourt Square: Prince Henry of Agincourt is thus remembered. The Royal Monmouthshire Royal Engineers, senior non-regular unit of today's army, occupy Great Castle House, inside the castle bailey.

(Open daily, at any time, throughout the year.)

RAGLAN CASTLE
(Off A40, midway between Monmouth and Abergavenny)

There was a castle on this site when the Normans were attempting the invasion of Wales, but what you see today is predominantly an early fourteenth-century hexagonal keep, the Great, or Yellow Tower, surrounded by its moat on the upper end of a fine site sloping down towards the Wilcae Brook. Though so much of this, and of the elaborately laid-out buildings to the north and west of it within the containing walls, was destroyed by the Parliamentarians at the close of the Civil War, enough has survived to give a strong and vivid impression of what Raglan was in its heyday.

North and west of the Great Tower are the two main courtyards, the Pitched Stone and the Fountain Courts. These are separated by the great hall, the chapel (curiously not orientated east-west), the long gallery and the lord's residence. They are bounded on each side by other extensive buildings: kitchen, buttery, pantry, office, and so on. Raglan was the administrative centre of a huge area and was designed to fulfil every function that might be required of it, especially during its occupation by the distinguished Herbert family. The beautiful Closet Tower to the east of the fine twin-towered gatehouse was probably the muniment room; it matches the beautiful Kitchen Tower to the north which in spite of its lowly name is, with its gun-ports set low in the hexagonal masonry, among the most notable of Raglan's main features.

But there are countless other, smaller features worth looking for: the slots in which the double portcullises operated; the pit for the counterbalance-weight on the drawbridge; the evident alteration to the door-jambs to the Closet Tower basement so that the former dungeon could be used to house barrels instead of prisoners; the rare 'batter' of the Great Tower; the ingeniously contrived newel staircase at the south gate and the buttery end of the main passage, set in the thickness of the walls. All these, and so many other interesting features, are to be seen and admired at Raglan. Though the main buildings have been so cruelly 'slighted' by the Parliamentarians, enough remains to indicate the spacious conception of the early fifteenth-century designers, and the glory that must have been in ample evidence throughout the fifteenth, sixteenth and early seventeenth centuries in which Raglan flourished.

(Open during standard hours, see p 8, and also Sunday mornings, from April to September.)

SKENFRITH CASTLE
(On B4521, 6 miles north-west of Monmouth)

This is one of a trio of border castles erected in the early thirteenth century along the west bank of the River Monnow, the other two being Grosmont and Llantilio ('White Castle') a few miles to the north and west in this part-Welsh, part-English 'hybrid' county. Like other such castles, they were built to protect English property and territory against Welsh aggression. All are well worth inspection, including Llantilio (or Llandeilo Groeseny), nicknamed 'White' because of the plasterwork that formerly characterised it. But the most impressive is Skenfrith, an irregular quadrilateral of massive curtain walls, 80 yards by about 50, forming a bailey containing a notable circular keep on a motte situated near the southern, narrower, end.

At each corner there is a substantial tower with embrasures cut so as to enable archers to enfilade the walls meeting it on each side. The main gateway was in the middle of the north wall and the keep was approached by a track hemmed in on each side by a moat and a bank which almost surrounded it within the bailey itself. The curtain walls were well protected on the east side by the river, and on the west and south sides by a moat originally more than 40 ft wide and reinforced with stone revetments, though little of this can now be seen. There was a system of sluices outside the south-east tower controlling the water in the outer moat, which was of course drawn from the river flowing at the foot of the east wall.

The motte is the usual cone shape, about 50 ft across at a height of 15 ft above the bailey. It once carried a timber stockade, and the stone wall now has an unusual feature: an excrescence on the west curve which originally housed a turret staircase linking the three storeys of the keep above a basement hollowed out of the motte itself. One of the upper floors formed the principal accommodation of the castle governor, though set against the south wall are the remains of what was either the great hall or the solar, which suggests that there was a period when Welsh aggression was sufficiently curbed for a more relaxed existence to be possible. Today, beneath its overshadowing trees, Skenfrith Castle is as quiet, as unaffected by the rush of modern life, as is the hamlet itself, so close beside its ancient walls.

(Open at all times throughout the year.)

ALNWICK CASTLE
(On A1, north side of the town of Alnwick)

Thirty miles south of the border town of Berwick-upon-Tweed, Alnwick ranks as the most important of the Border castles that, down the turbulent centuries, formed the strongholds of the northern chieftains continuously at war with the Scots. It has been the fighting base of the Percy family—whose name crops up so consistently in the Border Ballads—for seven centuries. It is still owned by the Duke of Northumberland.

Few English castles present such an immediately forbidding aspect. The early fifteenth-century barbican and gatehouse constitute one of the most perfect specimens of this classic feature extant. Two massive square towers flank the archway, supported immediately to the rear by another pair of equally massive octagonal towers; between the two pairs there was originally a deep moat spanned by a drawbridge, the marks of whose chains may still be discerned in the stonework on either side. The barbican and gatehouse are rendered even more menacing by the huge stone figures, as of sentries, perched in aggressive stances on top of the battlemented walls.

Beyond the gatehouse are the outer and middle baileys. Between them rises the main block of the castle buildings: the keep, the octagon towers, the chapel, the formidable central guard-chamber and other chambers built round the focal point, the inner bailey, a stone-locked courtyard where, after many centuries of bloodshed, the pulse at last beats quietly. The three baileys and their buildings are ringed about by an imposing array of fourteenth-century curtain walls and named towers: Constable's and Falconer's, Warder's and Avener's, Auditor's and Record. The successive generations of Percys, aware of the determination of their blood-feuding enemies from across the Border, left nothing to chance but made sure and doubly sure all round.

The townward face of the castle is grim, severe. But to the north-east it overlooks sloping, wooded park land, falling leisurely towards the River Aln. There could hardly be a stronger, more satisfying, contrast and it emphasises the point that the Northumbrian Percys can now live there at ease, surrounded by the treasures they have accumulated down the years, both warlike and otherwise, which are now displayed for the pleasure of the visitor to this most northerly-situated castle.

(Open May - 25 September daily, except Fridays and Saturdays, from 1-5.)

BAMBURGH CASTLE
(Off A1, 14 miles north of Alnwick)

Nearly two thousand years ago the Romans established a strong-point on the 150 ft high outcrop of basalt that frowns over the North Sea on the outskirts of the township of Bamburgh. The Angles had a fortified base here in the sixth century, walled with stone, which was attacked by the Danes a thousand years ago; for centuries it was a stronghold for a succession of warring Northumbrian chieftains.

It possesses a twelfth-century keep almost 70 ft square and all the more impressive because its height is only half its breadth. In an overall area of eight acres it contains three baileys. The original main entrance was through the west barbican, now in ruins; today entrance is by the east barbican, on the seaward side. An unusual sunken roadway leads from one bailey to another, appearing all the deeper because of the lofty walls towering on either side. In the east bailey there is a small chapel, as ancient as the keep itself. Inside the keep, which is buttressed by sturdy angle-towers, is the original water-supply: a well sunk through the solid basalt to the sandstone beneath at a depth of over 240 ft. It was discovered by chance during excavations two centuries ago. So thick are the walls of the keep that a straight staircase has been constructed in one of them, and there is the customary spiral stairway in the north-west angle too. Below the whole structure there is a vaulted basement storey, hewn out of the virgin rock.

Over the long centuries the castle changed hands many times, notably in the reigns of Edward IV and Henry VI. In 1463 it was taken and retaken over and again, but then fell on hard times. Two hundred years ago some parts of it were converted into granaries, against famine. Later, parts were adapted for use as a boarding-school for needy children. Still later, it served as a place of refuge for mariners shipwrecked off that treacherous coast; the top of the keep served as a lookout post and signal station for many years. It was off this headland that in 1838 Grace Darling and her lighthouse-keeper father rescued the crew of the 'Forfarshire'. Her grave and memorial, and a museum containing their little rowing-boat and other possessions, may be found only a few hundred yards inland from the castle.

(Open Easter to 30 September daily, including Sundays, from 2-8.)

NORHAM CASTLE
(Off A698, 8 miles south-west of Berwick-upon-Tweed)

This is one of the most famous of the Border castles. In 'Marmion', Scott wrote of its 'Embattled towers, the donjon keep, The loophole grates where captives weep'; its twelfth-century west gate is known to this day as Marmion's Gate, after the historic feat of Sir William Marmion during the siege of the castle by Robert the Bruce. Not surprisingly, a castle built in the early twelfth century and under continuous bitter attack by the Scots for hundreds of years, changing hands according to varying fortune, bears on such masonry as survives the brutal scars of that fighting.

The castle stands high above the south bank of the Tweed, overlooking a ford that was vital to both offence and defence, a few miles downstream of the medieval Twizel Bridge. An outer moat, fed from the river, protected its south and east sides; the river itself the north and west sides. Within lay the great outer ward, much of whose ancient walls are now almost at ground level. The west (or Marmion's) gate led into this, and thence to barbican and main gate giving access to the inner ward. Dominating the whole from its site in the south-east corner of the inner ward is the splendid ruin of the late-twelfth-century keep: a huge rectangular mass, 84 ft by 60, and 90 ft high. Externally, its 12 ft thick walls are in relatively good condition, but the interior has been largely gutted. However, corbels, fireplaces, arches and garderobes now give a clear picture of what this four-storey keep must have looked like in its heyday. Here King John received the homage of William the Lion. Some years later it was the stronghold of Edward I, and of Edward II during Robert the Bruce's successive sieges; later still, Edward III and Edward IV were there. In the intervals it was held by successive Bishops of Northumberland. In the fifteenth century the castle was involved in the Wars of the Roses; in the sixteenth century it fell to James IV of Scotland, who soon afterwards was defeated at nearby Flodden Field, so that it was again in English hands. Successive Governors during the endless Border Marches wars repaired and rebuilt its battered walls. But its giant scars remain and are, today, mute but honourable witness to four long centuries of almost unbroken involvement in the fiercest of Border strife.

(Open during standard hours, see p 8, throughout the year.)

WARKWORTH CASTLE

(On A1068, 7 miles south-east of Alnwick)

The ancient township of Warkworth is circled on three sides by the River Coquet, itself spanned by a noble medieval bridge. On a rocky eminence to the south of the town, also nearly encircled by the river, stands this splendid stronghold of the Percys, begun in the twelfth century, rebuilt and strengthened in the tumultuous centuries that followed: yet another Border castle designed to resist the turbulent Scots and serve the English, like Alnwick, Norham, Carlisle, Brougham and their many fellow castles.

The finest aspect is from the south, where you are confronted by the thirteenth-century curtain wall flanked by the Montagu and Carrickfergus Towers and, midway between them, the imposing thirteenth-century gatehouse and tower with its twin guardrooms and polygonal corner buttresses. There was formerly a drawbridge, backed by a portcullis, between them forming a trap for the invader, who could thus be fired on at point-blank range from both guardrooms at once. Immediately behind that lies the sloping outer ward, with the remains of hall, kitchen, chapel and stabling against the inner face of the curtain walls and, on the north side, the remains of a church built to serve a College of Secular Canons within the castle in a later century.

Beyond the church, standing proudly on the crest of the slope and towering above the steep banks that drop down to the Coquet far beneath, is one of the most elaborately designed of post-Norman keeps. Basically a square, with 65 ft sides, it has a tower protruding from each face, and is thus virtually eight-sided. The complex of eight towers rises through three storeys, with a 'lantern' passing through the centre from summit to base and a series of ingeniously contrived closets and stairways cut in the thickness of the outer walls. The upper storeys contain the lord's apartments, the great hall, solar and inner chamber, for this was both residence and stronghold combined, built and occupied by a proud clan that made its mark throughout Northumbria.

The castle is in fact a palimpsest of historic military architecture, from the twelfth-century walls by way of succeeding styles to some as recent at the sixteenth century. Very rarely is an ancient castle to be found that so perfectly complements a memorable site, like this one, high above the 'ox-bow' of the River Coquet.

(Open during standard hours, see p 8, and also Sunday mornings, from April to September.)

NEWARK CASTLE

The Romans' Fosse Way, running north-eastwards to Lincoln and beyond, crosses the Great North Road near its junction with the River Trent flowing north-eastwards to join the Ouse near Hull. It is on this strategic site, over-looking an important ford that was in time replaced by a succession of timber and later stone bridges, that some time in the early twelfth century the first stronghold was erected. Expert surveys have shown that there were probably at least three castles on the site from this date onwards, built to dominate the two main arteries that had by then replaced the very much earlier trackways. The earliest castle, probably of timber, was almost certainly occupied by the Bishop of Lincoln, who was also Lord of the Manor of Newark. Indeed, throughout its chequered and often obscure history, it has alternated between royal and high-clerical ownership and occupancy. It was not until the very late twelfth century that a stone castle replaced the timber one, on a mound heightened and flattened to carry walls and towers enclosing a bailey that was about one acre in extent.

Major rebuilding took place in the next and following centuries. The gate-way and west tower, undermined by the river running close beneath, had to be underpinned and strengthened. A north tower was built containing the notorious 'bottle'-type dungeon which can be inspected to this day. A new and important water gate was built; the vast hall, of which little remains today, was added to and embellished—evidence that this was a residential, not a solely military, establishment. The castle walls were 12 ft thick and rose to 70 ft above river level: sufficient deterrent, it is obvious, to any would-be invader, royal or otherwise.

It was in Newark Castle, in 1216, that King John died. Two years later, in the reign of Henry III, it had to endure its most destructive siege, and for the next hundred years or so no fewer than nine bishops occupied the castle in succession. After this, records of its fortunes become scanty for a surprisingly long time but it came back into the news, of course, when it played a leading part in the defence of this strongly Royalist town. During the siege, silver was melted down to be minted into coins; these 'siege coins' may be seen in the castle museum to this day.

(Open all the year. Grounds are public park. Crypt and dungeons, etc, may be visited by arrangement with the curator on the premises.)

LUDLOW CASTLE

So peaceful is the little town, so sleepy the countryside, that a castle of this magnitude seems wholly out of place. But Ludlow is a Border town situated in the Welsh Marches, and for many centuries the scene of bitter if intermittent strife between Welsh and English on either side of Offa's Dyke. Within thirty years of the Norman Conquest, Roger de Lacy chose this rocky eminence, whose base is washed by the River Teme flowing southwards and eastwards round the town, and threw up a giant keep, to be appropriately known down the years as The Great Tower, and a curtain wall and sundry smaller towers enclosing a bailey: a gesture towards aggression. Within the next century and a half, a more extensive curtain wall was thrown up to contain an outer bailey embracing the original inner bailey. Other towers and other buildings were established and elaborated for this was to be a major Marches strongpoint. However, during succeeding centuries the need for protection and a spring-board for offensive effort died down; new and more homely (but still sub-stantial) buildings were erected within the bailey, and Ludlow was gradually transformed from pure fortress to royal palace and earned for itself, in Tudor times, the title 'The Windsor of the West'.

Entry is by the twelfth-century gatehouse on the south-east side where immediately facing you is the giant keep. A spiral stone staircase leads to the top from which, among the battlements and turrets, you have a stupendous view out over the countryside. You look down on the circular Norman chapel in the inner bailey; on the Council Room in which, in 1634, Milton's 'Comus' was performed; on the chambers occupied by Prince Arthur after his marriage to Catherine of Aragon—who became Henry VIII's wife after Arthur's death; on Mortimer's Tower in the south-west corner; and on the grim Hanging Tower attached to the northern curve of the curtain wall, a name which speaks for itself. But the need for such buildings decreased as the centuries became less turbulent. In the Civil War Ludlow was held by the Royalists, and claims to be among the very last to surrender to the Parliamentarians. Thereafter, its fortunes declined and much of its fabric decayed. But, though in England, it became the property of the ancient Welsh family, the Earls of Powis, who own it to this day.

(Open April-September 10.30-1 and 2-dusk, daily including Sundays; during winter months from 10.30-4.30 on weekdays, Sundays by special arrangement.)

Shropshire

STOKESAY CASTLE
(Off A49, 7 miles north-west of Ludlow)

Stokesay is probably unique. Very strictly, perhaps, it is not so much a castle as a fortified manor house, but there is really no essential difference. Though you enter by way of a beautiful half-timbered and by no means fortified gate-house, situated on the east corner of the rectangular bailey, which dates only from the early seventeenth century, you are immediately confronted on the far side by a range of stone buildings of the late thirteenth and early fourteenth centuries. From the south tower, dating from about 1300 AD, to the north tower, dating from fifty years earlier, a range of stone buildings of similar date occupies the whole of the long western wall. Nowadays you can look out over the curtain wall enclosing the bailey, across the moat (now dry) to the pleasant Shropshire countryside stretching away into the distance; but those walls were formerly high, enclosing the spacious bailey and the buildings, and imparting a strong sense of security to Stokesay Castle's occupants.

Enormous stepped buttresses brace these buildings on the inner side, those on the polygonal south tower being especially massive and rising in no fewer than five steps. A passage-block links this tower with the solar and adjoining great hall, of roughly the same date. This last is flanked to the north by the other great tower, irregular in outline and older than the remainder of the block by half a century, though its upper floor is probably contemporary with the great hall. This tower is particularly interesting, and unusual, in that it is capped by a half-timbered storey supported on corbels not of stone but of massive oak timbering. It dates back to the fourteenth century: conclusive evidence of the skill of the carpenters and the excellence of the material in which they worked. Between the two towers the block of buildings, better preserved than many in other castles of like age, carries sharp gables and a fine tiled roof, heavy enough to call for the triple-stepped buttresses that are so notable a feature. Inside, the timber-work, particularly in the roof of the great hall, is as impressive in its way as the fine masonry of the towers. It is rare to find such excellent craftsmanship in two such contrasted materials, on one site; Stokesay Castle is memorable, perhaps above all else, for just this.

(Open all the year, daily except Tuesdays. In summer from 9-6; in winter from 9 till dusk.)

Somerset

DUNSTER CASTLE
(Off A39, 3 miles south-east of Minehead)

At the foot of Dunster's high street an approach road climbs steeply up a tree-clad mound, the Tor, on the summit of which a keep was built by William de Mohun immediately after the Conquest. Though this has vanished, there are traces still of his curtain wall which surrounded the bailey. Just to the north of this the present castle was built in the thirteenth century by a descendant of the first de Mohun; his gatehouse and other works survive to this day. The present owners, the ancient Luttrell family, acquired the castle from de Mohun nearly six centuries ago. At intervals the original medieval work was altered and elaborated. For example, in 1420 Sir Hugh Luttrell built the outer gatehouse, a splendid crenellated structure with an archway, beyond which is to be found the older gatehouse with its formidable iron-studded doors, the finest specimen of the de Mohun period. It was here that, in 1869, the skeleton of a 7 ft tall man, still manacled, was laid bare. It takes a discerning eye to distinguish between the original and the later work, for this has been kept homogeneous by a succession of enlightened owners, down to the present day; even in the nineteenth century, when so much ancient work was, as the people responsible thought, 'improved', Dunster Castle's tradition was maintained with integrity.

Nevertheless, it has had a chequered history. During the Wars of the Roses it changed hands twice. During the Civil War it held out gallantly against the Parliamentarians until it was forced to capitulate after a bitter six-months' siege. It narrowly escaped complete destruction instead of the usual 'slighting' but, fortunately for the visitor today, the then owner paid a huge fine and so was permitted to retain his property inviolate. Today it presents a magnificent exterior crowning a great hill and, once through its doors, the visitor is offered a wealth of historic treasure accumulated during more than five centuries of ownership by one enlightened family. It is a family whose name has dominated the village and surrounding countryside for generations. The notable Market Cross at the top of the village was erected by a seventeenth-century Luttrell and a Luttrell gave his name to the beautiful Luttrell Arms whose windows overlook the Cross and the gracious buildings lining the whole of the street.

(Open Easter, Whitsun and August Bank Holiday Mondays from 10.15-12.40 and 2.15-4.40; on Wednesdays and Thursdays in June; on Tuesdays, Wednesdays and Thursdays in July, August and September. From October to May, on Wednesdays from 2.15-3.30.)

NUNNEY CASTLE

(Off A361, 3 miles south-west of Frome)

Almost entirely screened by this tiny, sequestered village lying athwart a very minor road to the West Country, this little gem of a castle could easily be entirely missed; this would be a pity, for it is one of the least known and also most rewarding of all our minor castles. It is, in fact, a castle-in-miniature: small, compact, symmetrically designed, somehow Lilliputian—and therefore curiously endearing in aspect.

It was built almost exactly six centuries ago, in 1373, by a man who had seen castles of this type during service in France. Much later than traditional Norman, it has no inner or outer bailey, no curtain walls, not even a keep. It is a rectangle of massive stonework flanked at each corner by a huge drum-tower, the two end pairs being so close as almost to touch one another. They rise to over 50 ft, four storeys high; the linking walls contained three storeys only, comprising the great hall on the second floor and the solar and other private chambers above it. Near the summit of the four towers are to be seen the impressive corbels that once supported a parapet-walk right round the castle, below the level of the four topmost turrets. The whole is enclosed by a moat some 25 ft wide and 10 ft deep, itself contained within a bank. There was probably an exterior curtain wall to be breached before the moat was crossed (a reversal of Norman practice), but if so, the stonework has vanished into the fabric of the cottages and other buildings that now surround the castle —something that is unhappily found all too often in such cases.

Nunney did not see much active service. With the permission of Edward III it was crenellated by Sir John de la Mare, sometime Sheriff of Somerset, and remained in his family until, in the sixteenth century, it passed into the hands of Richard Prater. With the outbreak of the Civil War it was garrisoned by a handful of men of the Royalist cause and besieged by the Parliamentarians to whom it inevitably surrendered, cruelly battered by their abundant artillery. The north wall was violently breached, the huge jagged gap remaining the paramount reminder of the devastating attack. The effect on the observer is curious: it is as though a child's well-loved and long cherished possession had been ruthlessly destroyed, its life brought to an untimely end.

(Open during standard hours, see p 8, throughout the year.)

FRAMLINGHAM CASTLE

(Off B1120, 19 miles north-east of Ipswich)

Though it must rank among the smaller castles—its turf-rampart enclosure is only 300 yards in diameter and the area enclosed within the curtain walls only 100 yards by 70—this castle is particularly interesting because the discerning eye can pick out examples of its four distinct building periods, ranging from very early twelfth century to the eighteenth century. In 1101 AD Roger Bigod built on this low bluff, on the north side of the present township of Framlingham, a palisaded timber stronghold inside massive turf outworks. Half a century later his son Hugh replaced the timber with stone. Half a century after that, his son Roger threw up the high curtain walls and the thirteen interposed towers, all of which can be seen to this day. He also built the great hall and chapel, whose remains are on the east side of the bailey, facing the fine E-shaped Poor House against the west wall which was built much later, of mixed masonry and brick, and buttressed by two of the towers. The custodian lives in its south wing and draws his water from the old well just inside the main gateway on the south side of the bailey, as the original garrison used to do.

You can walk round the curtain wall, counter-clockwise, from Earl Roger Bigod's gate tower to the northern end of the bailey, crossing nine of the towers as you do so. Below, on your right, extends the turf-enclosed outer bailey; at the ninth tower you look over the lower court which can be entered by the ancient postern gate and the prison tower, the massive base of which was for centuries the castle dungeon.

An interesting feature to be noticed at these gates is the series of holes cut in the masonry to take the ends of the huge draw-bars that reinforced the oak doors. Unusually, there is no keep in the bailey, but there were once stables, barns, a granary and a Sergeant's Chamber, all probably of timber and thatch —which explains why they are no longer in evidence. An unexpected feature to be found here, notably above the gate tower, is a number of beautiful chimneys in ornamental carved brick. In fact, they are dummies, the work of sixteenth-century craftsmen employed specially by the Dukes of Norfolk, the illustrious Howards, who for many generations were the owner-occupiers of Framlingham Castle.

(Open during standard hours, see p 8, and also Sunday mornings, from April to September.)

ORFORD CASTLE
(Off B1084, 20 miles east of Ipswich)

But for a drawing dated 1600 portraying this castle as it was nearly four centuries ago, we could only guess at its original layout. The drawing shows a fine curtain wall, extra-mural battlemented towers, and a gateway on the south side. Today only the keen eye can locate the contours of the extensive earthworks which supported walls and towers; all the masonry has vanished—used, perhaps, in the building of Orford, nearby. But the keep remains, splendid as ever: not merely one of the most impressive in the country but, in fact, unique in shape and interior design and miraculously preserved.

It overlooks the low-lying, water-threaded landscape ending in the lighthouse on Orford Ness. This was the classic 'invasion coast' for the Danes and others. Henry II had the castle built as 'one of the bones of the kingdom', both to establish his authority among the East Anglian barons and to resist invaders at their point of entry. Walls and towers alone would have offered formidable resistance; the keep would have threatened them from many miles out to sea. It stood, and still stands, 90 ft high, neither rectangular like the early Norman keeps, nor cylindrical like those of the thirteenth century. Built in 1166, its 10 ft thick walls are polygonal, enclosing three main chambers almost 30 ft in diameter, the whole flanked by three enormous tower-buttresses nearly 20 ft across and themselves enclosing substantial rooms. Their battlemented turrets rise above the flat roof of the central tower (once pointed). There is no other of this kind, or scale, in the country.

A stone-lined well drops beneath the basement floor; in the thickness of the wall is the grimmest of underground cells that originally served as both cesspit and dungeon. In the west tower buttressing the main halls are the chapel, chaplain's chamber, royal apartments, kitchens and Constable's Chambers. In the huge south buttress is perhaps the most finely preserved stone spiral staircase in any castle, rising uninterrupted to the turret top and giving access to store-chambers and roof. Strangely enough, less than 200 years after it was built, Orford ceased to be militarily important so in 1336 Edward III bestowed it 'in perpetuity' to the first of a succession of Earls of Suffolk, as a gesture of royal generosity.

(Open during standard hours, see p 8, and also Sunday mornings, from April to September.)

FARNHAM CASTLE

(Off A31, 10 miles west of Guildford)

This castle is unusual in having been built by a bishop to serve as the residence of a line of bishops who succeeded one another in office for no less than 800 years. Medieval bishops owned estates that stretched from Taunton in Somerset, to London; Farnham was conveniently placed towards the eastern end of these vast estates so, in 1138, Bishop Henry of Blois constructed a motte and erected on it a tall tower, indicating firm possession. On the south-east side he erected domestic buildings: a bishops' residence, two chapels, courtyards, halls and offices. Throughout the Middle Ages these were occupied by a succession of bishops of Winchester. Viewed from the air, the layout curiously resembles a vast keyhole set within turf ramparts: the shell-keep, which soon (and inexplicably) replaced the original tower, forms the 'hole', the outbuildings the wedge-shaped cleft beneath it to take the wards.

It is, of course, the shell-keep that truly denotes the castle, and it is of outstanding interest even though its walls are now of such modest height. Instead of being perched on top of the mound it was so constructed as to encase the mound over a diameter of 150 ft with walls some 8 ft thick, braced by a series of turrets at the four compass-points. In the dead centre you will find the remains of the original tower: a massive square of 18 ft thick walls 50 ft long. They enclose the vital central feature, the well, but in this case it is no less than 13 ft in diameter. This square tower on the motte may have risen to 100 ft above ground level, though the existing shell-keep is only half that height at most, and only its entry tower, on the east side, still stands to its original height. As you pass through it, look out for the holes that took the massive drawbars, the portcullis slot and the overhead meurtrière, or 'murder-hole'.

Not surprisingly, Farnham was not much involved in war (though prepared for it) down the ages, but like so many of its more specifically military fellows, it became a pawn during the Civil War. It changed hands several times, eventually to be 'slighted' just to the north of the gatehouse. Then the bishops of Winchester moved into it again, and from that time onwards the castle was a residence rather than a fortress.

(Open during standard hours, see p 8, throughout the year.)

ARUNDEL CASTLE

There was almost certainly a castle on this commanding site in the days of King Alfred, but the monumental complex of greyish-white masonry set among trees to the north and east of this little town is substantially Norman, even though parts of it were rebuilt over the centuries as a result of a series of bitter sieges. It retains the basic features of the original, however: the double bailey like that of Windsor Castle; the huge keep standing on its motte at the northern end of the bailey, short of the tilting-yard; and the enormous circular towers, alternating with rectangular ones, heavily battlemented. The great keep, of course, is the most impressive feature of all.

The entrance is from the lower end; the thirteenth-century barbican is on the south-western side, below the slope up to the keep. Not far away is the inner gateway, known as Earl Roger's Tower after Roger Montgomery who built it four years after the Battle of Hastings, at which he had fought. It was built of local flint and squared stone and its noble archway has survived intact for almost exactly 900 years. The great circular keep which he built at the same time, to replace that of King Alfred, has walls 10 ft thick and 30 ft high; in its centre is the flight of steps that led down to the basement ammunition vault and dungeon. From the keep you gaze back towards the vast assembly of castle buildings, towers, turrets and walls massed at the lower end of this slope: everything is on the heroic scale.

The castle was conceived and built, as its site and construction emphasise, as a feudal stronghold; it was near enough to the coast to be a powerful threat to any invader. Not unnaturally its history has been a stormy one. Henry I captured it from its builder within forty years, and it then passed through a series of ownerships until the first of the long line of Howards, Earls of Norfolk, came into possession in the late sixteenth century. They have occupied it to this day, except for a short interval during the Civil War when it was held by the Parliamentarians—the marks of the cannon-balls that reduced it can be seen on its walls to this day. Beautifully and peacefully situated, it is the finest by far of the south coast castles, and is carefully preserved as the country seat of England's Premier Earl.

(Open April to mid-June on Mondays to Thursdays from 1-4.30; 23 June to 26 September on Mondays to Fridays, with Saturdays in August only, from 12-4.30.)

BODIAM CASTLE
(Off A229, 12 miles north of Hastings)

So clear and still are the waters of the wide moat encircling this almost perfect specimen of a medieval castle that its battlemented walls, huge corner drum-towers and crenellated turrets are serenely reflected in them. This is indeed a 'dream' castle: everyone's conception of what an ancient castle should be like. But unexpected, nevertheless, in this gentle East Sussex landscape. Why is it here? Because six centuries ago the nearby Rother was a tidal estuary up which enemy ships could sail twelve miles inland. So, in 1385 Sir Edward Dalyngrigge was commanded by Richard II to 'strengthen and crenellate' the manor house he had built for his retirement after his return from taking an active part in the war in France.

Almost a perfect square, Bodiam's walls are 150 ft long and over 40 ft high; each angle is bastioned by a drum-tower some 30 ft in diameter and rising a further 20 ft to its crenellations. Midway along each wall is a massive square tower; deep water washes the foot of walls and towers alike. The noblest of them all is the gateway tower, midway along the north wall, the central feature of one of the finest military façades in all England. It is approached by a causeway spanning the wide moat and interrupted by a curious octagonal stone-built 'island' midway along. Excavation has revealed that originally invaders had to approach the gateway right-handedly, so that their shield-arms were useless against the defenders' fire. Then there was the barbican; and then the deep-set gatehouse, flanked by towers with gun-ports and with no fewer than three successive portcullises to face. Immediately above these are machicolations through which boiling oil and quicklime could be jettisoned. The outer portcullis, last raised to admit the hated Parliamentarians, is still in position, its murderous dagger-points uncomfortably close overhead. You pass below it, through the gatehouse, to penetrate the shell.

It is still a noble shell, today. Gone are all but the relics of the lord's hall, great chamber, kitchen and retainers' quarters that once lined the four walls. The well, still full, survives in the south-west tower, and above it is the dove-cote, so vital in time of siege, with 200 of its nesting-sites still in evidence.

(Open all the year on weekdays, including Bank Holidays, from 10-7; closing time from October to March is sunset; April to September, also Sundays, from 10-7.)

PEVENSEY CASTLE
(On A259, 4 miles north-east of Eastbourne)

This remarkable site is the 'Anderida' of the Romans: like Portchester, 70 miles to the west, a strong-point established to resist Saxon invasion. Its 25 ft walls of sandstone and rubble, 12 ft thick, with their irregularly placed, enormous bastions, enclosed ten acres overlooking Pevensey Bay. When the Romans left in the fourth century, the walls began to decay and, a hundred years later, invading Saxons massacred the defending Britons.

In 1066 William the Conqueror's fleet anchored in the bay and he and his men marched inland to do battle with King Harold at Hastings. As always, he moved fast. He made over the Roman fortress to his half-brother, Robert of Mortain who selected the south-east corner of the elliptical site for his Norman castle. A wide ditch and timber stockade were soon replaced by curtain walls of stone enclosing an inner bailey dominated by a massive keep which was built against the south-east section of the original Roman wall. It is unusual in shape: a rectangle 55 ft by 30 ft internally, but having six large apsidal projections, one of which contains the well-shaft. Rebuilding and strengthening went on through successive reigns, and a century after the first building was begun, the castle was sturdy enough to thwart the siege tactics of Simon de Montfort in 1265, and also those of Richard II.

Intermittently, though, the castle was neglected, and dilapidation set in. Twenty years before the Spanish Armada it was being 'cannibalised' for building-stone, but when the Armada was sighted a battery was installed and one of the anti-Armada guns is still to be seen on the site. It had, however, a second period of potential glory. Nearly four centuries later, in 1940, the imminent threat of a Nazi invasion led to its being enlisted for defence. The towers of the inner curtain walls were reinforced with concrete, roofed, and transformed into block-houses and 'pill-boxes' for defence and offence. More 'pill-boxes' were constructed on the reinforced ruins of the keep, on the outer bastions and the Romans' western gateway, all carefully disguised to resemble centuries-old masonry. The US Army Air Corps, with the Canadians, installed radio-direction and other equipment; so, a 1,600-year-old Roman stronghold became a bastion against a twentieth-century threat of invasion.

(Open during standard hours, see p 8, and also Sunday mornings, from April to September.)

KENILWORTH CASTLE
(On A46, 5 miles north of Warwick)

This is the romantic castle familiar to all readers of Scott's novel, 'Kenilworth'. Inside the great oval of the perimeter wall built by King John may be found the site of the 'pleasaunce' laid out by Henry VIII, the outer and base courts, the remains of the chapel built by Henry III seven and a half centuries ago, and the giant keep. With a massive tower at each corner, the keep is a rectangle 100 ft long by 75 ft wide, with walls no less than 20 ft thick at their base. Completed 800 years ago, it is the oldest part of the castle.

A door leads into the keep through the fore-buildings on its west side. From this you pass westwards through the remains of the fourteenth-century kitchen and servery and thence to the great hall with its magnificent fireplaces and oriel window, the great chamber and the second chamber beyond. Over the early centuries of its existence, Kenilworth was gradually transformed from a Norman-type castle to a castle-palace fit for royal visits. These state chambers were where Henry V, VI, VII and VIII resided on these occasions. Elizabeth I, having presented Kenilworth to the Earl of Leicester, then announced her impending arrival. She stayed three weeks and the cost of entertaining her and her vast retinue almost broke Leicester's resources. Such gifts, he found (as did other royal favourites) could be severe liabilities!

The year 1649 was a bad one for Kenilworth. Parliament decreed that it should be 'slighted', and much of the curtain walling, part of the great keep, and other notable portions of the walls and buildings were deliberately blown up. The artificial lake that had washed the south-western curve of the perimeter wall was drained. Colonel Hawkesworth, the demolition engineer, appropriated Leicester's buildings for himself and left his associates to divide the remainder between them. Oddly enough, in the eighteenth century a colony of weavers from nearby Coventry moved in as 'squatters': you can seen to this day the marks where they installed their looms, a tacit reminder that fear of siege can disappear and 'swords be beaten into ploughshares'. But the grim keep still frowns over the inner bailey, and Lunn's Tower, Mortimer's Tower and Sainteowe Tower still raise their solid masonry to the skies.

(Open during standard hours, see p 8, and also Sunday mornings, from April to September.)

WARWICK CASTLE

The great walls and magnificent flanking towers, Caesar's Tower and Guy's Tower, soar splendidly above the waters of the River Avon which flow past their foundations far below; this is indeed one of the most glorious of our ancient castles and has been occupied for more than two centuries by the Earls of Warwick. This continuous occupation, following on the devotion of earlier owners, notably the great Beauchamp family in the fourteenth century, largely accounts for the excellent preservation of the castle. The fabric has been cherished, strengthened, elaborated and beautified almost continuously since it was first built, immediately after the Norman Conquest, on a site that still includes the Saxon 'Lady of Mercia', Ethelfleda's Mound. The first Earls of Warwick held it for their monarchs against rival barons; then the Beauchamps came into possession. To them we owe most of the outstanding features: the superb Caesar's Tower, built in the mid-fourteenth century, the gate tower, barbican and curtain walls, and impressive Guy's Tower, built towards the end of that century, the two most spectacular features of a castle rich in such architectural items.

Caesar's Tower soars from its foundations at river level to almost 150 ft, the dungeon carved out of rock at its base. The curtain wall is interrupted by the massive gateway, gatehouse and protective barbican before continuing towards the very similar Guy's Tower which rises nearly as high, polygonal in shape, its fifth storey ringed by machicolations through which missiles could discharged. There are two other, lesser towers: one named after the unfortunate Duke of Clarence, and the other the Bear, which contains one of the very few surviving examples of a medieval bear-baiting pit. From the parapets and turrets a fine view is obtained over the spacious bailey, with its range of medieval state and domestic apartments running along one wall.

History has been relatively kind to Warwick Castle since its involvement in the wars of Henry III and the continuous strife with rival Midlands barons. Unusually, it was a Parliamentary stronghold during the Civil War. It fell to the Royalists but was little damaged and was duly retaken, once and for all, by the second Baron Brooke, whose name survives, three centuries later, in the family still happily in residence.

(Open April to mid-October on weekdays from 10-5.30 and on Sundays from 1-5. From October to March: Mondays to Fridays, and Sundays, from 12.30-4.30, and Saturdays from 10.30 to 4.30. Closed throughout December.)

BROUGH CASTLE
(Off A66, 8 miles south-east of Appleby)

Two thousand years ago the Romans recognised the importance of this site, the strategic gateway to the Pennines, and established a northern stronghold, Verterae, on the Stainmore track. For centuries this was a trade route linking Ireland's copper resources with the bronze-age communities of northern Europe. The Romans duly left and, not surprisingly, the Normans later recognised the value of the site and built a castle within the earth ramparts and moat which are the sole remaining evidence of Roman occupation. The castle we see today replaces the eleventh-century one built by William II and destroyed by William the Lion of Scotland in 1174. For a time it was a royal castle: Edward I and Edward II both stayed there. It survived the destruction of the township of Brough in the fourteenth century, and in due course passed into the hands of the famous Clifford family. The south-eastern corner drum-tower, built by the first Lord Clifford in 1300, was named after him and is notable for the elaborate pattern of the base on which it was erected. Sadly, some four or five centuries later much of it was demolished—simply to repair a nearby mill.

Only the northern part of the Roman site has been used. Here is the bailey, at the south-east end of which are the remains of the castle buildings, including the great hall, which occupied most of the space between the original gatehouse and Clifford's Tower. At the opposite, western end is the keep which Countess Anne always referred to as the Roman Tower, perhaps because it replaced an earlier keep built on the foundations of the Roman barracks. Evidence of successive building periods is emphasised by the presence of herringbone stonework, especially in the lower courses.

The keep, it is true, does not rank among the finest surviving post-Norman ones and but for the intelligent care of Lady Anne Clifford there might be little of it in evidence today. It contained the usual basement store-room, a large chamber above this, and the lord's private apartments, the solar, on an upper floor. Above this is a leaded 'fighting-deck' from which a magnificent view extends in all directions: beyond Swindale Beck which skirts one side of the castle, out and over the ruggedly beautiful expanse of the Pennines to which Brough was always the vital key.

(Open during standard hours, see p 8, throughout the year.)

BROUGHAM CASTLE
(Off B5288, 1 mile south-west of Penrith)

This is one of a notable quartet of northern castles that includes also Pendragon, Appleby and Brough. Like the latter, it is immensely old, being originally (as its former name, Brocavum, suggests) a Roman fort. The remains of that spacious but long-abandoned fort are still to be seen close by, guarding the crossing of the River Eamont, vital to the legionaries serving under Agricola in the first century AD. Their road ran north to Carlisle and Scotland, and south to Chester.

Brougham is particularly noteworthy because here no fewer than ten successive building periods may be seen in addition to the hint of Roman work. You enter the castle at the north-east corner, pass through the thirteenth-century outer gate and turn left into the complex mass of the towering twelfth-century keep, strangely known as the Pagan Tower. When you have climbed to the second storey you will find a most unusual feature: the tombstone of a Roman soldier, built into a passage-wall. The keep overlooks a triangular inner courtyard round which, in varying states of preservation, are the remains of the great hall, kitchen, chapel, great chamber, retainers' lodgings and other offices, abutting on to the thirteenth-century Tower of League in the south-west angle. Curtain walls and towers are enclosed by earth banks through which, in days gone by when the castle was under attack, there ran a wide moat.

Most closely associated with Brougham was the long-lived Lady Anne Clifford, who devoted her life to its elaboration and preservation. She died in a third-storey room of the inner gatehouse in 1676 when she was almost ninety —a great age for those days. On the south wall of the gate hall situated between outer and inner gates is a stone slab she erected to record her work for the castle. Opposite, a doorway leads through to a vaulted guardroom and, beneath this, to a deep-cut room that was the castle dungeon. Not many years after Lady Anne's death her good work was undone and much of the castle fell into disrepair. But for all that, the casual visitor today will be impressed by what he sees, and by its silence above the waters of the Eamont River; the specialist and connoisseur in castles will find Brougham a profitable hunting-ground for studying successive periods of military architecture.

(Open during standard hours, see p 8, throughout the year.)

CONISBROUGH CASTLE

(On A630, 5 miles south-west of Doncaster)

Even if the curtain walls surrounding the bailey had remained as massive as they must have been when they towered above these earthworks in the late twelfth century, they would have been entirely dwarfed by the magnificence of the great keep that stands proudly at their north-east corner, the work of Hamelin Plantagenet, half-brother to Henry II. There are larger keeps and older keeps, but Conisbrough's yields pride of place to none in originality and splendour of conception. And because, most happily for us, Conisbrough seems to have avoided involvement in warfare after the early fifteenth century, this keep, which might so well have been largely destroyed, still retains its twelfth-century outward splendour to captivate as well as dominate. There is no other keep like it in plan anywhere in the country.

It is a giant cylinder of stone whose curved walls rise to almost 90 ft in height and are 15 ft thick. As though this were deemed not enough, the cylinder is close-flanked by six buttresses: buttresses so enormous that each is a square tower in itself. They rise higher than the cylinder they embrace, to terminate in finely proportioned turrets. So huge are they that one of them contains an oratory, or small chapel; another contains a pigeon-loft; another a huge oven; yet another, two cisterns to hold water drawn up from the well beneath the base of the central tower. The whole vast edifice stands high on its earthworks overlooking the countryside in all directions. It has towered there for almost 800 years.

There is little evidence of other buildings within the encircling walls; the keep was self-contained, as well as being the focal point of the whole. A long flight of steps between the two south buttresses (one of which contains the oratory) gives access to the interior, level with the original wall-walk. The lower floors were used for storage and the well-head. The lord's chamber, with its own garderobe, or latrine, and fireplace, was above this, with a wash-basin in the thickness of the wall. Above it was the lord's retiring-room, or bedroom, again with a fireplace. In the uppermost portion you can see the corbels that originally supported the top-floor room, immediately beneath the conical roof that topped the cylindrical portion of the keep.

(Open during standard hours, see p 8, throughout the year.)

MIDDLEHAM CASTLE
(Off A6108, 2 miles south of Leyburn)

Most Norman and post-Norman castle builders utilised sites on which still earlier, Saxon or other, timber forts had stood. Middleham is an exception. It was begun a century after the Norman Conquest, on a site a quarter of a mile to the east of a much more ancient earthwork, the great keep being, as so often, the first part to be built. With 12 ft thick walls respectively 100 ft and 80 ft long, rising three storeys high, it ranks among the largest in England; it is perhaps even more imposing today, now that the thirteenth-century curtain walls and towers have largely crumbled away. These originally formed a rectangle some 250 ft along each side with a tower at each angle, the whole enclosed by a wide ditch. A drawbridge spanned this to give access to the gatehouse at the north-eastern corner of the bailey, an early fourteenth-century structure complete with guard-chamber flanking it to the east and also rising to three storeys in height.

There is not much left today of the buildings that must once have been set against the inner face of the curtain walls: the garrison's quarters, kitchens, cellars and store-rooms. But there are the remains of hearths and ovens and —an unusually rare and interesting feature—midway along the south wall a sixteenth-century horse-mill. It occupied the central part of an area that once contained another very rare feature, a 'Nurssee', or nursery; in this, according to tradition, Richard of Gloucester's son Edward played; he is generally believed to have been born in the adjacent south-west angle tower, the Prince's Tower, and to have died there too.

As so often in the less elaborately designed castles, the keep was both major stronghold and living accommodation also. It contained the great chamber on the first floor, above the ground-floor cellars; also the kitchen and curiously named Chamber of Presence on the west side of the longitudinally divided structure. There is a turret on both the south and the west sides, and a chapel on the east, also rising through three storeys. One of the turrets originally incorporated a dovecote, that all-important domestic feature in these isolated stronghold residences. Today a strange sense of loneliness pervades keep and bailey, bereft of their encircling curtain wall.

(Open during standard hours, see p 8, throughout the year.)

RICHMOND CASTLE
(Off A1, 12 miles south-west of Darlington)

An aerial photograph would reveal that, unlike the majority of medieval castles, this one is triangular in plan. It would also reveal that much of it is in ruins. Nevertheless, its magnificent eleventh-century curtain walls, among the oldest in the country, enclose it handsomely along the precipitous slopes that drop almost vertically 100 ft down to the River Swale below. You may follow a tree-shadowed path beneath these towering walls, looking down on the water glinting far below. Once through the gateway, you will see some of the finest eleventh- and twelfth-century masonry extant, most notably in the magnificent late-Norman keep.

Alan Rufus ('The Red'), son of Odo, first Constable of Dover Castle and himself first Earl of Richmond, fought alongside William the Conqueror. His earldom, and the duty of developing this castle, was his reward for valour and devotion. He built first a castle of timber and earthwork but then set about replacing the timber by stone. The noble 100 ft high keep, with its 11 ft thick walls, is a fine example of the Norman tradition in English castle building. Unhappily, the barbican, usually among the most impressive features of these castles, has fallen into near-ruin; but many lengths of the curtain walling still survive and some at least of the original mural towers. Among these are the Gold Hole Tower, with its persistent tradition of gold buried beneath its footings, waiting to be recovered. Another is the Lion Tower, named because after his defeat at the Battle of Alnwick in 1174 William the Lion, King of Scotland, was incarcerated there. It is three storeys in height, its barrel-vaulted bottom storey constituting the Chapel of St Nicholas.

There is a strangely romantic atmosphere about this castle, one that befits the feudal township spread out beneath its walls, notable for its spacious cobbled market square. It is firmly believed, locally, that though Richmond is a far cry from Tintagel in Cornwall, yet the legendary King Arthur and his Knights of the Round Table sleep beneath the solid stone of the 100 ft keep, ready to arise when the call comes for them to do so, and once again to prove their mettle. Pure fancy, may be, but traditions die hard, and one should not meet them with undue scorn, even today.

(Open during standard hours, see p 8, and also Sunday mornings, from April to September.)

SKIPTON CASTLE

On the north side of this old market town there is a huge mass of rock whose northern face drops 100 ft sheer down into the gorge of Haw Beck. It is this commanding site that was chosen, in the very early fourteenth century, for a castle to defend Mercia against Northumbria. It would be a fanatically determined enemy who scaled the vertical rock face and then the bastions of masonry that capped it. The more vulnerable east, south and west approaches were protected by a semicircular moat.

You enter by way of the great gatehouse on the south side, flanked by two drum-towers. Across the arch, carved in huge letters of stone, is DESORMAIS, the motto of the ancient Norman family, the de Cliffords, who provided no fewer than fourteen Lords of the Honour of Skipton between 1300 and 1675 AD. Translated, it is 'Henceforth', and as the castle's history reveals over four centuries, the motto was pregnant with meaning. Beyond the gatehouse lies the castle itself: a noble assemblage of high and solid walls enclosing a five-sided bailey and reinforced by a series of drum-towers that match those of the gatehouse in sturdiness; one of them is appropriately named the Watch Tower. So massive are the walls and towers that during the Civil War Sir John Mallory, with a garrison of no more than 300 men, sustained a siege by the Parliamentarians for three long years, and Cromwell is said to have regarded the castle as his most formidable challenge in the North. When at length they capitulated the garrison was granted permission to march out fully armed and with their band playing. Then, as usual, the castle was 'slighted' by the triumphant Roundheads.

There is nothing grim about Skipton Castle. Thanks particularly to Lady Anne, last of the long line of Cliffords, who obtained permission to repair the damage ten years after the 'slighting', and to her successors, it is in a notable state of preservation. There is much to be seen: the spiral staircase, the great baking hearth and even larger whole-ox roasting hearth, and Lady Anne's Entrance on the west side, which she designed herself. And do not miss the beautifully preserved Conduit Court in which you will find, still flourishing, a 300-year-old yew tree, which contributes a breath of life to a pageant of history here nobly enshrined in stone.

(Open all the year, except Good Friday and Christmas Day, from 10 till sunset on weekdays and from 2 till sunset on Sundays.)

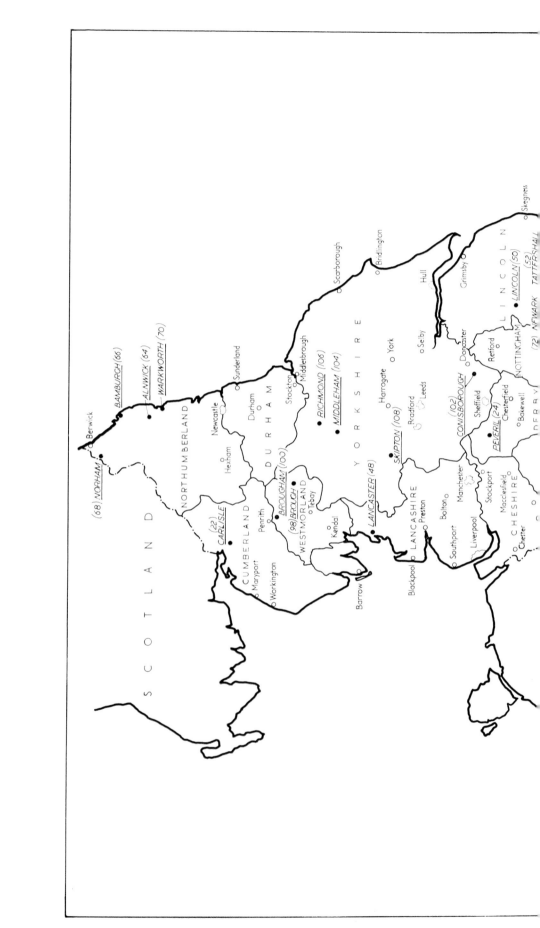

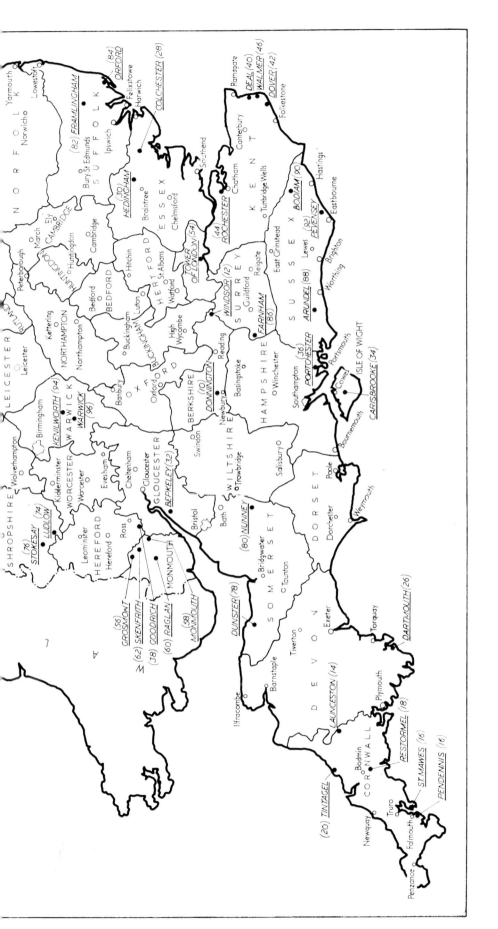

NORFOLK
Yarmouth
Lowestoft
Norwich

(82) FRAMLINGHAM
(84) ORFORD
Felixstowe
Harwich
SUFFOLK
Ipswich
Bury St Edmunds

COLCHESTER (28)

HUNTINGDON
Peterborough
March
Ely
CAMBRIDGE
Huntingdon
Cambridge

(30) HEDINGHAM
Braintree
ESSEX
Chelmsford
Southend

RAMSGATE
Ramsgate
DEAL (40)
WALMER (46)
DOVER (42)
Folkestone

Canterbury
Chatham
KENT
Tunbridge Wells
Hastings
Eastbourne

ROCHESTER (44)

BODIAM (90)
PEVENSEY (92)

LEICESTER
Leicester
RUTLAND

NORTHAMPTON
Kettering
Northampton

BEDFORD
Bedford

HERTFORD
Hitchin
St Albans
Watford
Luton

TOWER OF LONDON (54)

WINDSOR (12)
SURREY
Guildford
Reigate
East Grinstead

SUSSEX
Lewes
ARUNDEL (88)
Brighton
Worthing

KENILWORTH (94)
Birmingham
Wolverhampton
WARWICK (96)

WORCESTER
Kidderminster
Worcester
Evesham

SHROPSHIRE
STOKESAY (76)
LUDLOW (74)

HEREFORD
Leominster
Hereford
Ross

BERKELEY (32)
GLOUCESTER
Cheltenham
Gloucester

OXFORD
Banbury
Oxford
BUCKINGHAM
Buckingham
High Wycombe

BERKSHIRE
Swindon
Reading
Newbury
DONNINGTON (10)

WILTSHIRE
Bath
Trowbridge
Salisbury

FARNHAM (86)
HAMPSHIRE
Basingstoke
Winchester
Southampton

PORTCHESTER (36)
Portsmouth
Cowes
ISLE OF WIGHT
CARISBROOKE (34)

NUNNEY (80)

SOMERSET
Bristol
Bridgwater
Taunton

DORSET
Poole
Dorchester
Weymouth
Bournemouth

GROSMONT (56)
SKENFRITH (62)
GOODRICH (38)
RAGLAN (60)
MONMOUTH (58)
MONMOUTH

DUNSTER (78)

DEVON
Ilfracombe
Barnstaple
Tiverton
Exeter
Torquay

DARTMOUTH (26)

LAUNCESTON (14)
Plymouth

CORNWALL
Bodmin
Newquay
Truro
Falmouth
Penzance

TINTAGEL (20)
RESTORMEL (16)
ST MAWES (16)
PENDENNIS (6)

Glossary of architectural terms used

Bailey (or Ward)	Enclosed courtyard
Barbican	Protective extension to a main gateway
Berm	Level between base of wall and inner slope of ditch
Corbels	Projecting stones designed to support roof or parapet
Crenellation	Gaps left in parapet for firing and observation
Curtain wall	Wall enclosing bailey and/or other parts of castle
Donjon	Keep or Great Tower, often, but not always, containing the dungeons
Drawbridge	Timber bridge across moat, capable of being raised and lowered either by ropes or chains, or by counter-balance
Embrasure	Splayed opening in outer wall for observation and firing
Fore-building	Protective building against keep forming means of entry
Garderobe	Latrine, normally in thickness of outer wall
Keep (or Great Tower)	Usually the strongest single feature in a castle (see Donjon)
Machicolation	Series of gaps between corbels supporting rampart, through which missiles could be discharged downwards on enemy
Motte	Mound (artificial or natural) used as base of early castles
Portcullis	Iron-shod timber grille suspended in grooves in front of gateway, let down by chains as additional protection or trap
Postern	A minor gateway, usually at rear, set in curtain wall
Quoin	A corner stone at angle of building
Solar	A withdrawing-room adjacent to upper end of a hall, used by the lord and his family and honoured guests
Ward (or Bailey)	Enclosed courtyard